FIRST WATCH

STORY FARM

WINTER PARK • MIAMI
SANTA BARBARA

FIRST WATCH

YEAH, IT'S FRESH

SOME OF OUR FAVORITE RECIPES FOR BREAKFAST, BRUNCH AND LUNCH

PHOTOGRAPHS BY JON WHITTLE

Yeah It's Fresh: Some of Our Favorite Recipes
for Breakfast, Brunch and Lunch

Published in the United States of America
by Story Farm, Inc.

Library of Congress-Cataloging-in-Publication Data
available upon request.
ISBN 978-0-9969441-8-2

FIRST WATCH

PROJECT MANAGEMENT Cari Trimyer, ACME BRAND STUDIO
CULINARY DEVELOPMENT Shane Schaibly, Scott Nuss

STORY FARM

EDITORIAL DIRECTOR Ashley Fraxedas
CREATIVE DIRECTOR Jason Farmand
FOOD STYLISTS Katie Farmand, MacKenzie Smith
COPY EDITORS Karen Cakebread, Laura Paquette
INDEXING Amy Hall
PRODUCTION MANAGEMENT Tina Dahl

Printed in the United States of America

10 9 8 7 6 5 4
Fourth Edition 2022

This book is dedicated to our customers and employees. You're the reason we wake up very early and very happy every morning.

FIRST WATCH
BREAKFAST • BRUNCH • LUNCH

CONTENTS

GOOD. MORNING.

WELCOMING YOU to this cookbook is a lot like welcoming you to one of our restaurants: Come on in. Make yourself comfortable. And let us share some First Watch goodness with you.

We've spent close to four decades laying the groundwork for *Yeah, It's Fresh: Some of Our Favorite Recipes for Breakfast, Brunch and Lunch*. The stories and recipes you'll find here span generations and trace their roots to Pacific Grove, California, between Monterey and Carmel-by-the-Sea, where our first restaurant opened in 1983, and Sarasota, Florida, the picturesque town on the Gulf of Mexico, which we have called home since 1986. We opened that original restaurant in Pacific Grove in a space that was once a factory that made tin cans for the area's thriving sardine fishery. Funny, but we've never been tempted to put those tiny, briny fish on our menu.

Founder John Sullivan, an Arizona native, and his friend Ken Pendery, who hails from Kentucky, worked together at a couple of restaurant groups before setting out to create a place of their own with a shared vision of what their ideal restaurant should be. Long before "farm-to-table" became a culinary mantra, Sullivan and Pendery committed themselves to launching a casual gathering spot where guests could enjoy meals made from the freshest ingredients available, with everything prepared in-house whenever possible.

"We didn't set out to be a 'healthy restaurant,' per se. After all, we had pancakes, waffles and biscuits on the menu," says Pendery. "But we were sticklers for freshness and we always will be. Find the best eggs. Find the best bacon. Find the freshest of everything. And when you find the best and the freshest, then healthy just naturally follows. The healthy label stuck to us and we've more than lived up to it. We're proud of that."

From the beginning, there was another crucial part of the First Watch equation: People. Pendery and Sullivan knew too many folks in the restaurant industry who were forced to balance the grueling hours dictated by their careers against spending time with their families. They believed there was a better way.

"We wanted to provide a place where talented professionals could do great work and not have to pull a shift where they came home at one o'clock in the morning," says Sullivan. "Heck, Ken and I didn't want those crazy hours either."

Which explains why we've stuck to breakfast, brunch and lunch. We open at 7 a.m., close at 2:30 p.m., and everyone has a life.

As for the restaurant's name? It came about when Sullivan was working on renovations at that old cannery.

"It was early in the morning and I was pounding nails into a beam, gazing out at the sailboats on Monterey Bay. We'd been trying to come up with a nautical name, one that had two simple syllables," says Sullivan. "Thinking about the crews on those boats heading out at the crack of dawn, well, First Watch just kinda popped into my head. Then I went back to pounding nails."

fresh
EGGS
DAD'S
Soquel, CA

THAT ROLL-UP-your-sleeves-and-enjoy-the-work ethos remains part of the DNA at First Watch. While we've grown to more than 200 locations across the United States and our menus have changed with the times, we still do things the way we did them in Pacific Grove. We slice our own fresh fruit. We whip up our batters from scratch. We juice our own juices. We make eggs to order. And if diners ask for it, we're happy to cook something for them that's not on our menu.

In other words, it's home cooking on a grand scale.

THROUGHOUT OUR history, we've kept our ear close to the ground when it comes to food trends. During the 1980s and much of the 1990s, our innovative-at-the-time menu didn't stray all that far afield from its origins. But all that changed with the foodie explosion of recent years and the growing culinary sophistication of our guests. When guests began requesting things like organic greens, cage-free eggs and all-natural chicken, we rose to the occasion and found partners who could provide us with fresh, top-quality products on a consistent basis. Remember life before quinoa? First Watch was the first national restaurant group to put quinoa on its menu (although we did have to spell it out phonetically and explain what it was). It's now one of our more popular ingredients, and you'll find it in everything from our Power Breakfast and Chicken Pesto Quinoa Bowls (pages 117 and 118) to our Lemon Blueberry Quinoa Pancakes (page 82).

While we keep tabs on the burgeoning food scene, we know better than to hop on every culinary bandwagon that comes along. We also know that when it comes to breakfast, brunch and lunch, our guests don't want too many surprises. So, we study the trends, decide what has staying power, and then introduce it in the form of our seasonal offerings, like Avocado Toast (page 69) and the Elevated Egg Sandwich (page 90), both of which ultimately made it to our daily menu.

FIRST WATCH CULINARY team members often hit the road on one of their frequent "Culinary Inspiration Tours," where they visit cities across the U.S., immerse themselves in the local food scenes and find inspiration for our ever-evolving menu.

Likewise, we hope the recipes on these pages will inspire you to cook our favorite dishes. Because just like when you're eating at First Watch, you'll know that, yeah, it's fresh.

GOOD TASTE STANDS THE TEST OF TIME

Fruity Chicken/Fruity Tuna
Greek Salad
Cobb Salad
Bleu Nut Spinach Salad
"YOU FIRST"
We will.
First Watch
First Watch
FirstWatch
THE DAYTIME CAFÉ
FIRST WATCH
BREAKFAST · BRUNCH · LUNCH
FIRST WATCH
THE DAYTIME CAFE
- WE PROUDLY FEATURE FRESH SEASONAL PRODUCE FROM LOCAL GROWERS WHENEVER POSSIBLE -
CLASSIC FAVORITES
THE TRADITIONAL BREAKFAST Two fresh cage-free eggs* any style with your choice of bacon, smoked ham, turkey sausage or pork sausage links. Served with whole grain artisan toast, all-natural house preserves and fresh, seasoned potatoes. 9.79
TRI-FECTA Two fresh cage-free eggs* any style with either a light and airy Belgian waffle or a multigrain pancake. Plus your choice of bacon, turkey sausage or pork sausage link. 9.79
THE HEALTHIER SIDE
EGG-SCLUSIVES
OMELETS AND FRITTATAS
FROM THE GRIDDLE
POWER BOWLS

FIRST WATCH ESSENTIALS

We believe the perfect breakfast, brunch and lunch doesn't have to be fancy or complicated. It comes from practice, proper techniques and wholesome, fresh ingredients, like our Traditional Breakfast (pictured on page 14)—cage-free eggs served with crispy bacon and perfectly seasoned potatoes. So we dedicated this entire first chapter to just that: these core things that make First Watch great. From the perfectly cooked egg to hard-searing potatoes, our house seasoning blend to deliciously roasted vegetables, here are the First Watch ESSENTIALS.

EGG COOKING 101

Cooking eggs is a very gentle art. They're fragile, can go from perfect to overdone in a matter of seconds and they leave very little room for error. In fact, if you ever want to test someone's culinary chops, simply ask them to make you an omelet. But fear not—we're here to help you master the task.

We cook our eggs in nonstick pans over VERY high heat using a single flip method; at home, however, we recommend starting the eggs in an unheated pan with a little bit of oil or melted butter, then cooking over medium heat, as you have more time and you will have much more control this way.

We used to teach the flip method by using an English muffin in a pan and having cooks flip it from one side to the other, over and over again. It takes a gentle toss and an ever-so-slight drop of the pan to soften the blow when the eggs hit the pan on the landing. The flip is a great way to impress your friends, but it takes confidence and a bit of practice. You may also use a large, flexible spatula that will slide under the egg and support most of the egg as you turn it over. Cooking eggs well is something that can be greatly satisfying and will help raise your aspirations in the kitchen.

OVER EASY

Crack 2 eggs into a cup. That allows you to make sure you don't break the yolks and to pick out any shell. Carefully pour eggs into a buttered, nonstick, nonheated pan. Turn heat on to medium. Watch carefully as whites begin to set, about 3 minutes. Then flip carefully so yolks don't break and cook for 1 additional minute. Over-easy eggs should have a very runny yolk, and some of the white around the yolk should still be soft.

OVER MEDIUM

Begin an over-medium egg the same way as an over-easy egg, but after you carefully flip the egg, let it cook for an additional 3 minutes. Over-medium eggs should have a runny yolk, but the white around the yolk should be solid and completely cooked.

OVER HARD

Begin an over-hard egg the same way as an over-easy egg, but once eggs are in the pan, break the yolks and cook until the entire egg is solid throughout. Do not disturb or move the egg around while cooking, as this will result in a scrambled egg. Once cooked through, flip and cook for an additional 3 minutes.

SUNNY SIDE UP

Place 2 eggs in a buttered, nonstick, nonheated pan and cook over medium-low heat. This gives the heat more time to cook the bottom of the eggs while not overcooking the yolks and browning the edges of the eggs. Cook for about 3 minutes or until desired firmness.

BASTED

Place 2 eggs in a buttered, nonstick, nonheated pan and cook over medium-low heat. This gives more time to cook the bottom of the eggs while not overcooking the yolks and browning the edges of the eggs. Add 1 tablespoon of water and cover with a lid for about a minute, giving a beautiful finish to the eggs. This creates a "skin" over the top of the yolks so they appear white instead of yellow; however, they will still be runny.

POACHED

Heat a small pot half full of water with about ¼ cup of white vinegar. The technical poaching temperature is 160°F to 180°F. A simmer happens at 180°F to 200°F and a boil at 212°F. You don't want to be in the simmer or boiling world if you're trying to poach eggs! Once you get your temperature right, spin the water with a wire whisk or spoon to create a whirlpool in the water and crack the eggs in one at a time. Cook over medium-high heat for about 3 minutes or so, then use a slotted spoon to remove them. You may cook longer for a well-done or hard-poached egg.

WHIPPED

This preparation works great for omelets and frittatas. Use a whisk or hand blender to mix cracked eggs in a bowl until frothy. You can mix ahead of time and store in an airtight container and refrigerate, but the best way is to whip just before adding them to the pan. This will guarantee that the air you've just whipped in will result in a nice fluffy finished product. Add whipped eggs to a buttered, nonstick, nonheated pan and cook over medium-low heat. Work with a rubber spatula by pushing and pulling the edges to create big ridges. When eggs are cooked, finish folded or open faced.

SCRAMBLED

We make scrambled eggs from whole eggs mixed in the cooking pan. Break 2 eggs into a buttered, nonstick, nonheated pan and cook over medium-low heat, continuously stirring with a rubber spatula. As the eggs cook, take care to continuously move the eggs around with the spatula. Keep the spatula touching the bottom of the pan and continue until the eggs are mostly cooked and have a nice glossy sheen. Serve immediately.

MILLION DOLLAR BACON

If you thought bacon couldn't get any better, try this winning formula. It's sweet and salty and spicy and absolute perfection. The key is to make sure to whisk the cayenne, black pepper, brown sugar, syrup and water together well, so that you get a little bit of everything in each bite. We think this bacon makes the perfect side, topper on deviled eggs and garnish in a Bloody Mary. But we certainly understand if you order it as your entree.

MAKES 8 SLICES

FOR MILLION DOLLAR BACON GLAZE

1 cup brown sugar

1 tablespoon black pepper

1 teaspoon cayenne pepper

½ cup maple syrup

½ cup water

FOR BACON

8 slices bacon

PREPARE MILLION DOLLAR BACON GLAZE

Whisk sugar, black pepper, cayenne pepper, syrup and water together in a large bowl. Set aside.

FINISH BACON

1. Preheat oven to 325°F. Place a roasting rack on a sheet pan lined with parchment paper.
2. Drag slices of bacon through glaze mixture and place on prepared sheet pan.
3. Bake for 15 minutes. Rotate pan and cook for another 5 minutes, making sure not to overcook.
4. When bacon is cooked to desired crispiness, set aside until ready to serve.

FIRST WATCH POTATOES

Good potatoes are as important to any breakfast as perfectly cooked eggs and crispy bacon. We prefer large Russet Norkotah potatoes, peeled and diced into big cubes. One of our kitchen secrets is to parboil the diced potatoes until they are barely soft but still have texture. This will cut your cooking time down tremendously. Then, to finish, make sure to have plenty of oil in your skillet and give the potatoes a hard sear on all sides. Color is key! From the color comes all the flavor. We add sweet onion and First Watch seasoning—it's that simple.

SERVES 1

- 1 pound potatoes, diced into ½-inch pieces
- ½ cup onions, julienned
- 1 tablespoon First Watch Seasoning (page 26)
- 2 tablespoons canola oil

1. Bring 3 quarts of salted water to a boil. Add diced potatoes and cook for approximately 10 minutes, or until just al dente.
2. Drain potatoes and immediately plunge into 3 quarts of ice water to stop cooking. Stir occasionally and strain potatoes from ice water once completely cooled (about 5 minutes).
3. In a mixing bowl, combine potatoes with onions.
4. Sprinkle seasoning over potatoes, add oil and toss well, ensuring potatoes are evenly coated with oil and seasoning.
5. Heat an electric griddle or nonstick pan over high heat.
6. Add potatoes and cook for 4½ minutes. Be careful not to crowd the pan, as you won't get proper browning.
7. Use a rubber spatula to mix potatoes, separating the browned sides from the griddle and mixing with uncooked potatoes.
8. Continue to cook for an additional 4½ minutes (for approximately 9 minutes total to be fully cooked and ready to serve).

LEMON WHITE BALSAMIC VINAIGRETTE

MAKES ABOUT 4 CUPS

- ½ cup water
- ¼ cup mustard
- ¼ cup lemon juice
- 2 tablespoons white balsamic vinegar
- 1 tablespoon kosher salt
- ½ tablespoon granulated sugar
- ½ teaspoon black pepper
- ½ teaspoon granulated garlic
- 4 cups canola oil
- ¼ cup green onions, finely sliced

1. In a mixing bowl, combine all ingredients except oil and green onions. Whisk/blend together to incorporate.
2. Slowly add oil to liquid mixture to incorporate, whisking/blending the entire time.
3. Add finely sliced green onions and mix well.
4. Store in an airtight container in the refrigerator.

– NOTE –

A hand or immersion blender is the perfect tool for this dressing, but you can also use a wire whisk. Just make sure you have even and steady whisking so that the oil is incorporated and forms an emulsion with the other ingredients.

FIRST WATCH SEASONING

MAKES ALMOST 3 CUPS

- 2 cups kosher salt
- ½ cup black pepper
- 1 tablespoon garlic powder
- ½ tablespoon onion salt
- 1½ tablespoons paprika

1. In a mixing bowl, combine ingredients thoroughly to evenly distribute.
2. Place in an airtight storage container and store in a dry place.

– NOTE –

This is our house recipe for the seasoning blend we use in many of our recipes. It's a secret, so shhhh . . . don't tell anyone! If you don't have these ingredients available, plain kosher salt and fresh cracked pepper will work just fine. We also encourage you to create your own "house blend" based on your preferences: a little more garlic, a little less pepper, whatever you happen to have in the cabinet. Just make sure you have about 50 percent kosher salt in the final version.

ROASTED CRIMINI MUSHROOMS

PAGE 30

ROASTED ZUCCHINI

PAGE 31

ROASTED ONIONS

PAGE 31

ROASTED TOMATOES

PAGE 32

ROASTED VEGETABLES

At First Watch, we take great pride in the fact that we cut and roast our fresh vegetables in house every day. Taking the extra time and energy to roast vegetables makes all the difference in our recipes and, ultimately, in our food. Roasting brings out natural sweetness and adds color and char to the vegetables, which, in turn, adds a new layer of dimension to each dish. When roasting, always use a convection oven and be careful not to cut the vegetables too small. It's easier to get that beautiful, deep color on larger pieces. You'll also want to be careful not to overcook them, as you want to maintain texture and not turn them into mush. We season the veggies prior to roasting, so you won't want to add too much salt or pepper after the roasting process.

ROASTED CRIMINI MUSHROOMS

MAKES ABOUT 4 CUPS

2½ pounds whole crimini mushrooms

¼ cup canola or olive oil

½ tablespoon First Watch Seasoning (page 26)

– NOTE –

To turn our Roasted Crimini Mushrooms into Caps, Etc., a favorite dish that was on our menu when we first opened, simply top the mushrooms with melted shredded cheddar jack cheese and serve with 2 eggs, potatoes and an English muffin.

1 Preheat oven to 375°F.
2 In a mixing bowl, combine mushrooms, oil and seasoning and toss until mushrooms are evenly coated.
3 Line a sheet pan with parchment paper and transfer the contents of the bowl onto the pan, spreading mushrooms evenly across the surface.
4 Bake for 10 minutes, until mushrooms are golden brown.
5 After mushrooms are cool, cut them into quarters if diameter of the cap is larger than a quarter, and in half if smaller than a quarter. Set aside until ready to use.

ROASTED ZUCCHINI

MAKES ABOUT 4 CUPS

2 pounds zucchini, diced (about ½ to 1 inch thick)

1 tablespoon canola or olive oil

½ tablespoon First Watch Seasoning (page 26)

1 Preheat oven to 375°F.
2 In a mixing bowl, combine zucchini, oil and seasoning and toss well until zucchini is evenly coated.
3 Line a sheet pan with parchment paper and transfer the contents of the bowl onto the pan, spreading zucchini evenly across the surface.
4 Bake for 10 minutes. Stir, using a rubber spatula, and bake for 10 more minutes.
5 Remove from oven and cool.
6 Store zucchini in an airtight container and refrigerate until ready to use.

ROASTED ONIONS

MAKES ABOUT 4 CUPS

2½ pounds onions, ¼-inch julienned

2 tablespoons canola or olive oil

½ tablespoon First Watch Seasoning (page 26)

1 Preheat oven to 375°F.
2 In a mixing bowl, combine onions, oil and seasoning and toss until onions are evenly coated.
3 Line a sheet pan with parchment paper and transfer the contents of the bowl onto the pan, spreading onions evenly across the surface.
4 Bake for 15 minutes. Stir, using a rubber spatula, and bake for another 15 minutes.
5 Remove from oven and cool.
6 Store onions in an airtight container and refrigerate until ready to use.

ROASTED TOMATOES

MAKES ABOUT 4 CUPS

5 pounds Roma tomatoes, cut lengthwise and deseeded

¼ cup canola or olive oil

½ tablespoon First Watch Seasoning (page 26)

1 Preheat oven to 300°F.
2 In a mixing bowl, combine tomatoes, oil and seasoning and toss well until tomatoes are evenly coated.
3 Line a sheet pan with parchment paper and transfer the contents of the bowl onto the pan, spreading tomatoes evenly across the surface with cut sides facing up.
4 Bake for 45 minutes. Rotate pan in oven and bake an additional 15 minutes, until skins start to shrink and turn golden brown.
5 Cut each tomato half into sixths. Set aside until ready to use.

ROASTED SHALLOTS

MAKES ABOUT 8 CUPS

1½ pounds whole shallots, peeled

2 tablespoons canola or olive oil

1 tablespoon First Watch Seasoning (page 26)

1 Preheat oven to 375°F.
2 Slice shallots in half lengthwise, then place flat-side down on a cutting board and cut into ¼ inch slices.
3 In a mixing bowl, combine shallots, oil and seasoning until shallots are evenly coated.
4 Line a sheet pan with parchment paper and transfer the contents of the bowl onto the pan, spreading shallots evenly across the surface.
5 Bake for 7 minutes. Stir, using a rubber spatula, and bake for 7 minutes more. Set aside until ready to use.

FIRST WATCH GRANOLA

MAKES ABOUT 8 CUPS

6 cups rolled oats

1 cup sunflower seeds, roasted, salted

2 cups wheat germ

1½ cups almonds, slivered

1 tablespoon cinnamon

1 cup maple syrup

½ cup brown sugar

½ cup canola oil

¼ cup agave syrup

2 tablespoons vanilla extract

– NOTE –

To add another layer of flavor, feel free to add about 1 to 2 cups of your favorite dried cranberries or dried cherries after the granola has cooled completely.

1 In a large mixing bowl, combine oats, sunflower seeds, wheat germ, almonds and cinnamon; mix ingredients two times to distribute cinnamon evenly.
2 In another mixing bowl, combine maple syrup, brown sugar, oil, agave and vanilla. Mix using a wire whisk. Pour over dry ingredients.
3 Using a rubber spatula or your hands, mix into granola until all dry ingredients are evenly coated.
4 Split mix evenly on 2 greased sheet pans. Spread out the mix in a single layer on both trays. Do not press granola down.
5 Bake at 300°F for 20 minutes. When golden brown, remove from oven and cool completely at room temperature.
6 Once granola is completely cool, break into ideal-sized pieces (about the size of a quarter).
7 Transfer to an airtight container and store in a dry place for up to 1 week.

EGGS & OMELETS

BACADO OMELET

This omelet is a great example of how quality ingredients combine to make the perfect dish. It's super simple and has been on our menu since day one. We bake our bacon on parchment paper in a really hot oven, which ensures a perfect cook every time. Be sure to let the bacon cool for at least 10 minutes before dicing, otherwise it won't be crispy.

SERVES 1

FOR PICO DE GALLO

6 Roma tomatoes, diced small

1 cup cilantro, roughly chopped

1 jalapeño, deseeded and minced

Juice of 1 lime

1 teaspoon kosher salt

FOR OMELET

1 tablespoon butter

¾ cup Whipped Eggs (page 21)

¼ cup crispy bacon, diced into ½-inch pieces

4 avocado slices

2 tablespoons Monterey Jack cheese, shredded

2 tablespoons sour cream

Pico de Gallo (recipe above)

PREPARE PICO DE GALLO

1. Place all ingredients in a mixing bowl and toss to combine.
2. Store in an airtight container in the refrigerator.

PREPARE OMELET

1. In a 10-inch nonstick pan, heat butter over medium-high heat to lightly coat pan, then add eggs.
2. As soon as the bottom surface of the eggs has started to set up as the base of the omelet, work with a rubber spatula by pushing and pulling the edges to create big ridges. Continue until the omelet is still slightly wet.
3. Separate the edges of the omelet from the pan with the spatula and add bacon and 3 slices of avocado, one at a time, evenly over the top half of the omelet (from 9 o'clock position to 3 o'clock position) to ensure there is bacon and avocado in every bite. Sprinkle with cheese.
4. When cheese has melted, remove pan from heat. Carefully fold the bottom half with no ingredients over the top half with ingredients. Top with a pinch of crisp bacon, one slice of avocado and sour cream.
5. Transfer to a plate and serve with a small side of Pico de Gallo.

CHILE CHORIZO OMELET

Chorizo was not found on most menus when First Watch opened its doors in 1983. But we loved the snappy flavor it imparted and made it the star of this omelet. This Mexican-inspired dish has all of our favorites—roasted onions, Pico de Gallo, avocado and cheese. These days chorizo is more common, but this omelet is anything but.

SERVES 1

1 tablespoon olive oil

1 medium-sized fresh poblano pepper, deseeded and diced small

1 tablespoon butter

¾ cup Whipped Eggs (page 21)

¼ cup cooked chorizo, crumbled

3 avocado slices

1 tablespoon Roasted Onions (page 31)

2 tablespoons cheddar jack cheese, shredded

OPTIONAL ACCOMPANIMENTS

2 tablespoons sour cream

2 tablespoons Pico de Gallo (page 36)

1. In a 10-inch nonstick pan, heat olive oil over medium-high heat to lightly coat pan, then add poblano peppers. Cook until softened and lightly browned, about 5 minutes. Transfer to a small plate and set aside until ready to use.
2. In another 10-inch nonstick pan, heat butter over medium-high heat to lightly coat pan, then add eggs.
3. As soon as the bottom surface of the eggs has started to set up as the base of the omelet, work with a rubber spatula by pushing and pulling the edges to create big ridges. Continue until the omelet is still slightly wet.
4. Separate the edges of the omelet from the pan with the spatula and add chorizo and 3 slices of avocado, one at a time, evenly over the top half of the omelet (from 9 o'clock position to 3 o'clock position) to ensure there is chorizo and avocado in every bite. Sprinkle with poblano peppers, onions and cheese.
5. When cheese has melted, remove pan from heat. Carefully fold the bottom half with no ingredients over the top half with ingredients. Top with a pinch of diced poblano peppers.
6. Transfer to a plate and serve with sour cream and Pico de Gallo on the side.

HAM & GRUYÈRE OMELET

In keeping with the First Watch philosophy of doing things differently, we kicked the normal Swiss cheese out of our ham omelet and added a young Gruyère—both inside the omelet and on top—which gives it an earthy nuttiness. We source ours from one of the only suppliers of Gruyère in the United States, deep in the heart of Wisconsin. We also use freshly shaved deli ham instead of diced ham inside the omelet, which we feel adds a certain luxury to the finished dish.

SERVES 1

- 1 tablespoon butter
- ¾ cup Whipped Eggs (page 21)
- 2¼ ounces cooked ham, shaved
- 2 slices Gruyère cheese
- Freshly chopped parsley, for garnish
- Freshly chopped chives, for garnish

1. In a 10-inch nonstick pan, heat butter over medium-high heat to lightly coat pan, then add eggs.
2. As soon as the bottom of the omelet has started to set, work with a rubber spatula by pulling the edges toward the center and allowing uncooked egg to run underneath the cooked areas. Continue until the omelet is still slightly wet.
3. Separate the edges of the omelet from the pan with the spatula and spread ham evenly over the top half of the omelet (from 9 o'clock position to 3 o'clock position) to ensure ham in every bite.
4. Add a slice of Gruyère cheese. Fold in half and top with the other slice of Gruyère cheese.
5. Transfer to a plate and top with fresh herbs.

MORNING MARKET VEGETABLE OMELET

We roast all of our vegetables in-house, so they add a depth of flavor to our omelets that really sets them apart. The other key to this dish is just keeping it simple. It's not about the sauces or garnishes; it truly is all about the roasted vegetables. Though the herbed goat cheese deserves a salute, too.

SERVES 1

- 1 tablespoon butter
- ¾ cup Whipped Eggs (page 21)
- 2 tablespoons Roasted Crimini Mushrooms (page 30)
- 1 tablespoon Roasted Zucchini (page 31)
- 2 tablespoons Roasted Shallots, (page 32)
- ¼ cup kale, cut into thin strips
- 1 tablespoon Roasted Tomatoes, (page 32), plus extra for garnish
- ¼ cup herbed goat cheese
- Freshly chopped parsley, for garnish
- Freshly chopped chives, for garnish

1. In a 10-inch nonstick pan, heat butter over medium-high heat to lightly coat pan, then add eggs.
2. As soon as the bottom of the omelet has started to set, work with a rubber spatula by pulling the edges toward the center and allowing uncooked egg to run underneath the cooked areas. Continue until the omelet is still slightly wet.
3. Separate the edges of the omelet from the pan with the spatula and layer vegetables evenly over the top half of the omelet (from 9 o'clock position to 3 o'clock position) to ensure there are vegetables in every bite. Finish with goat cheese.
4. Carefully fold the omelet's bottom half (with no ingredients) over the top half (with ingredients).
5. Transfer to a plate and top with fresh herbs and remaining tomatoes.

– NOTE –

To make a fresh, delicious herbed goat cheese, add about ½ cup each of chopped chives and parsley to about a pound of goat cheese.

SONORAN FRITTATA

Given our California roots, Mexican flavors and ingredients influenced much of our original menu. This frittata is one of our most popular legacy dishes, thanks to that triple whammy of spicy chorizo, sweet onions and fresh Pico de Gallo. A little secret—while the Sonoran Frittata is no longer on our menu, we're happy to make one if you order it. And we'll know you're a longtime First Watcher.

SERVES 1

- 1 tablespoon butter
- ¾ cup Whipped Eggs (page 21)
- 1 tablespoon Roasted Onions (page 31), diced
- 2 tablespoons cooked chorizo, crumbled
- ¼ cup Pico de Gallo (page 36)
- ¼ cup cheddar jack cheese, shredded
- 2 tablespoons sour cream

1. In an 8-inch nonstick pan, melt butter over medium-high heat, then add eggs.
2. Add onions and chorizo, and when the frittata begins to set, cook it like an omelet, lifting sections with a rubber spatula and letting the uncooked egg run underneath the cooked areas.
3. When the frittata is two-thirds cooked, after about 2 minutes, flip and continue to cook for 1 minute more.
4. When the frittata is set, flip back and top with Pico de Gallo and cheese.
5. Transfer to a plate and top with sour cream.

SMOKED SALMON & ROASTED VEGETABLE FRITTATA

1 tablespoon butter

1 ounce Smoked Salmon, sliced (page 49)

¼ cup Roasted Shallots (page 32)

2 tablespoons Roasted Tomatoes (page 32)

¾ cup Whipped Eggs (page 21)

1 tablespoon Parmesan cheese, shredded

2 tablespoons Chive Cream (page 64)

Freshly chopped parsley, for garnish

Freshly chopped chives, for garnish

– NOTE –

These recipes are for a single frittata. To serve more, the ingredients can simply be doubled or tripled based on the size of your pan and how confident you are in your frittata flipping skills!

There's just something about smoked salmon and eggs that, when combined in this easy frittata, comforts the soul. And the shallots add a surprising sweetness to the dish. For perfect roasted tomatoes, remove the seeds and roast the tomato halves cut-side up. This releases the liquid so you don't wind up with stewed tomatoes.

SERVES 1

1. In an 8-inch nonstick pan, melt butter over medium-high heat.
2. Add salmon, shallots and tomatoes and sauté for 1 minute, until warm throughout.
3. Add eggs and gently stir with a rubber spatula, pushing cooked eggs toward the center and allowing uncooked egg to run underneath the cooked areas, for about 45 seconds.
4. Add cheese and stir briefly.
5. When almost completely set, flip frittata in pan and cook for an additional 45 seconds.
6. Flip again, transfer to a plate and serve with Chive Cream and fresh herbs.

SMOKED SALMON

1½ cups brown sugar

2 tablespoons garlic powder

2 tablespoons kosher salt

2 teaspoons black pepper

2 salmon fillets, about 2 pounds each

1 In a bowl, combine brown sugar, garlic powder, salt and pepper.

2 Sprinkle half of the rub into a shallow dish, then place salmon fillets on top. Sprinkle rest of rub on top of the fish and let salmon sit in the refrigerator for up to 8 hours. The rub will be almost liquid by the time it is done.

3 Preheat a smoker to 165°F.

4 Pat salmon dry with a paper towel, then place both fillets in a smoker.

5 Smoke on low heat for about 1 hour, making sure to maintain the 165°F temperature.

6 Carefully remove from smoker and set aside. Cool to room temperature and then wrap with plastic wrap and continue chilling overnight in a refrigerator.

7 Salmon is ready to slice the next day and slices best when cold.

JOAQUIN YAHOO

This frittata is a vegetarian's dream. But with loads of house-roasted vegetables, fresh mushrooms, whipped eggs and Pico de Gallo, meat lovers need not despair. Frittatas were some of our original signature dishes and were not found on many other menus in the late '80s. This version was named after the San Joaquin Valley in California, near where our restaurant first planted its roots. We like to keep the names of our dishes light, fun and close to home—just like our food.

SERVES 1

- 1 tablespoon butter
- ¾ cup Whipped Eggs (page 21)
- 1 tablespoon Roasted Zucchini (page 31)
- 1 tablespoon Roasted Onions (page 31)
- 1 tablespoon kale, cut into thin strips
- 1 tablespoon Roasted Crimini Mushrooms (page 30)
- ¼ cup Pico de Gallo (page 36)
- 2 tablespoons cheddar jack cheese, shredded
- 2 tablespoons sour cream

1. In an 8-inch nonstick pan, melt butter over medium-high heat, then add eggs.
2. Add veggies, and when the frittata begins to set, cook it like an omelet, lifting sections with a rubber spatula and letting the uncooked egg run underneath the cooked areas.
3. When the frittata is two-thirds cooked, after about 2 minutes, flip and continue to cook for 1 minute more.
4. When the frittata is set, flip back and top with cheese and Pico de Gallo.
5. Transfer to a plate and serve with sour cream on the side.

BLT BENEDICT

Benedicts require a tiny bit of finesse, but are totally worth the effort. The key is homemade Hollandaise Sauce, so avoid store-bought if at all possible. We bump up the lemon in our sauce, letting the acid play nicely against the richness of this dish.

SERVES 1

FOR HOLLANDAISE SAUCE

4 egg yolks

1 tablespoon lemon juice, fresh

½ cup unsalted butter, melted

½ teaspoon hot sauce

¼ teaspoon salt

FOR BENEDICT

1 half slice ciabatta bread (about 6 x 3 inches)

2 slices crispy bacon

2 slices fresh tomato (beefsteak or large heirloom)

2 Poached Eggs (page 20)

¼ cup Hollandaise Sauce (recipe above)

½ cup arugula

1 tablespoon Lemon White Balsamic Vinaigrette (page 26)

2 avocado slices

Freshly chopped parsley, for garnish

Freshly chopped chives, for garnish

PREPARE HOLLANDAISE SAUCE

1 Whisk egg yolks and lemon juice together vigorously in a small stainless-steel bowl and place over a pan of simmering water (180°F to 200°F).

2 Continue to whisk, making sure eggs do not get too hot or they will begin to cook.

3 Slowly add melted butter, whisking vigorously the entire time, until sauce doubles in volume.

4 Remove from heat; add hot sauce and salt. Keep warm until ready to serve.

PREPARE BENEDICT

1 Toast ciabatta until brown. Top with bacon and tomato.

2 Place eggs on top of tomato, then top with Hollandaise Sauce.

3 In a separate bowl, combine arugula and dressing. Set aside.

4 Top benedict with lemon-dressed arugula, avocado slices and fresh herbs and serve.

– NOTE –

Arugula is a delicate green, so don't add the dressing until just before serving or the greens will wilt.

EVERYTHING SMOKED SALMON BENEDICT

What sets our benedicts apart is that we don't use English muffins. Instead, we opt for more flavorful ciabatta bread, which, like an English muffin, has lots of nooks and crannies to soak up all that Hollandaise Sauce goodness. Ciabatta also offers a certain sourness that takes our benedicts to a whole other level. Just be sure to have plenty of everything bagel spice on hand, since this dish is a definite crowd pleaser.

SERVES 1

- 1 half slice ciabatta bread (about 6 x 3 inches)
- 2 tablespoons whipped cream cheese
- 2 ounces Smoked Salmon (page 49)
- 2 Poached Eggs (page 20)
- ¼ cup Hollandaise Sauce (page 53)
- 2 tablespoons red onions, julienned
- 2 tablespoons toasted everything bagel spice

1. Toast ciabatta until brown. Top with whipped cream cheese and Smoked Salmon.
2. Place eggs on top of salmon. Top with Hollandaise Sauce and onions, and sprinkle everything bagel spice over both eggs.

– NOTE –

To toast the everything bagel spice blend, sprinkle the seasoning on a rimmed baking sheet and cook for about 6 minutes at 350°F. This will bring out the garlic and onion flavor.

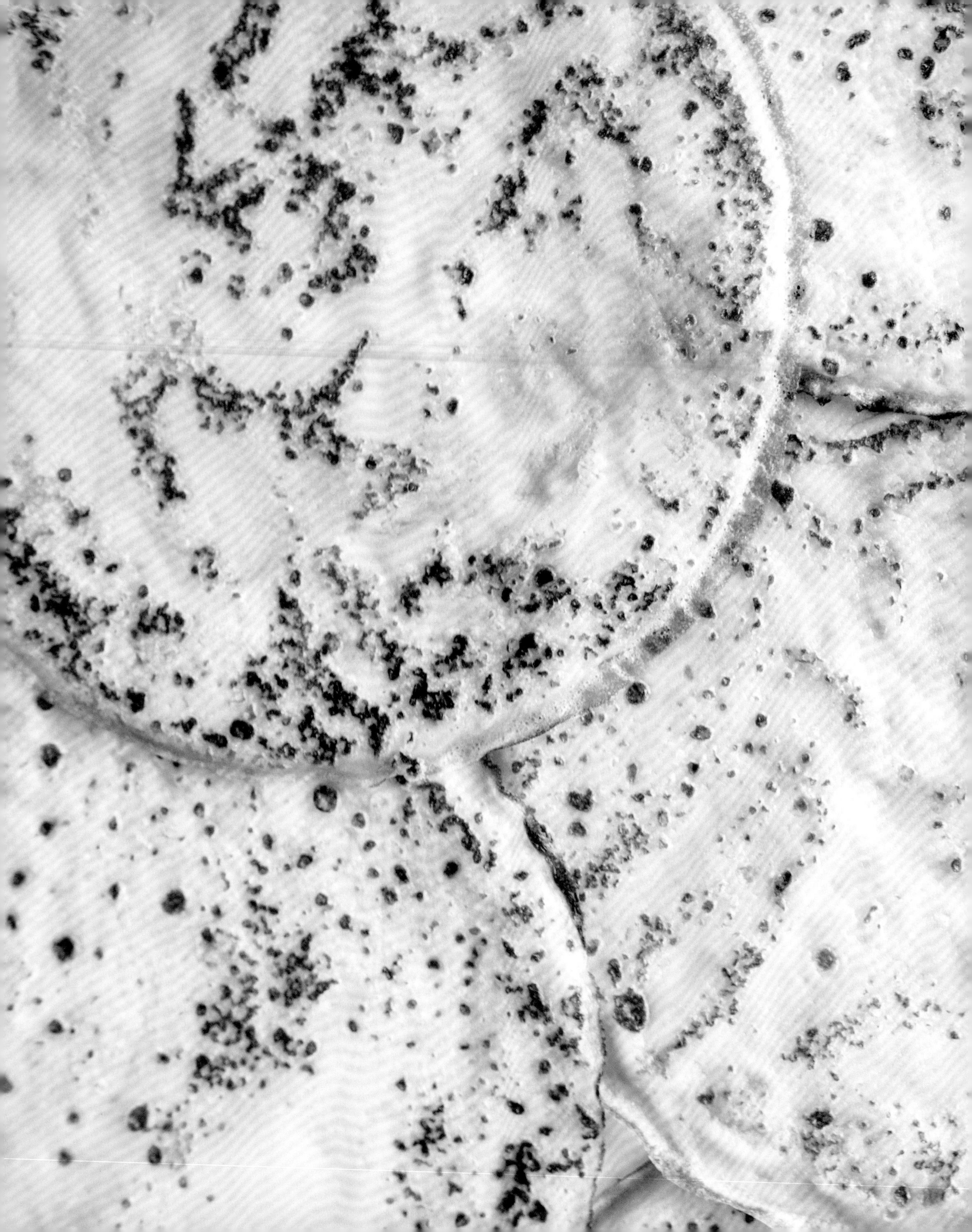

CREPE EGGS

Our crepe eggs are the perfect combination of sweet and savory all wrapped up in one. And you don't need a fancy crepe maker. We use a 10-inch omelet pan. Making crepes is all about the wrist roll. Get the pan hot, ladle the batter into one quarter of the pan and gently roll the pan in a circular motion to let the batter cover the surface. Practice makes perfect, which isn't a bad thing when it involves eating lots of delicious crepes. These crepes can be used to make one—or all—of our signature crepe egg dishes, or simply rolled around fruit for a sweet treat.

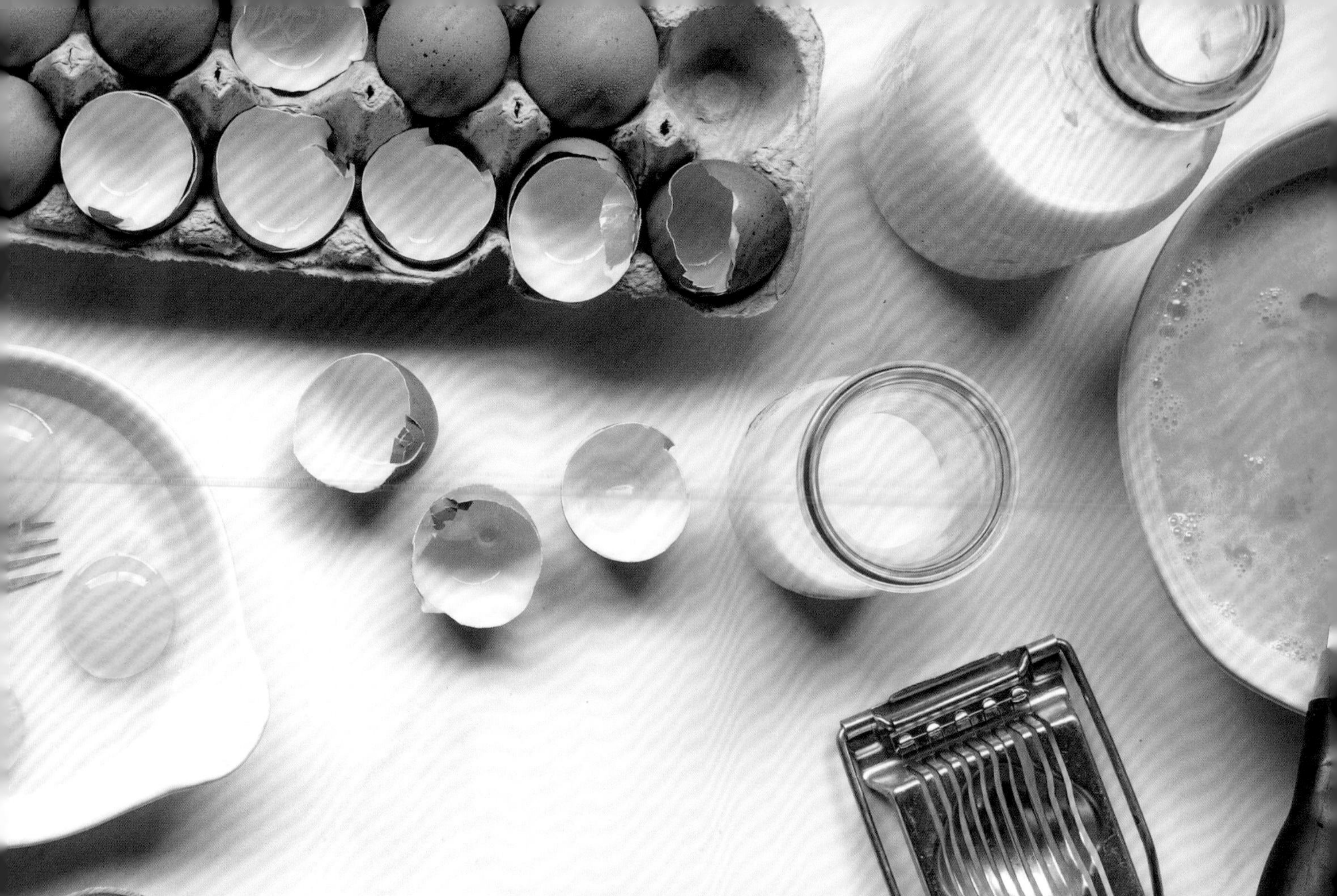

CREPE BATTER

MAKES ABOUT 8 CREPES

- 1¼ cups flour
- 1 tablespoon powdered sugar
- ½ teaspoon kosher salt
- 2¼ cups milk
- ½ cup Whipped Eggs (page 21)
- ½ tablespoon canola oil
- ½ tablespoon vanilla extract

1. In a mixing bowl, carefully measure and combine the first 3 ingredients.
2. In a separate bowl, measure all remaining ingredients and whisk to blend.
3. Combine all ingredients and mix well.
4. Heat a 10-inch nonstick pan and ladle ¼ cup of batter into bottom of pan.
5. Cook on medium heat until batter settles and edges begin to brown. Flip over and cook the other side until the crepe moves freely in the pan. Store on a plate, covered with plastic wrap, until ready to serve.

TURKEY DILL CREPE EGGS

SERVES 1

- 1 Crepe (page 58)
- ¼ cup Whipped Eggs (page 21)
- ¼ cup cooked turkey, diced
- ¼ cup baby spinach
- 2 tablespoons Roasted Crimini Mushrooms (page 30)
- ¼ cup Monterey Jack cheese, shredded
- ¼ cup Hollandaise Sauce (page 53)
- 5 sprigs fresh dill

1. Preheat a 10-inch nonstick pan over medium-high heat.
2. When pan is hot, add crepe and immediately add eggs, making sure surface of the crepe is covered.
3. Add turkey, spinach and mushrooms, again making sure the entire crepe is covered. Sprinkle with cheese.
4. Crepe is done when it can slide freely in the pan.
5. Fold in half and top with Hollandaise Sauce and fresh dill.

CALIFORNIA CREPE EGGS

SERVES 1

1 Crepe (page 58)

¼ cup Whipped Eggs (page 21)

¼ cup cooked ham, diced

2 tablespoons Roasted Onions (page 31)

2 tablespoons Roasted Crimini Mushrooms (page 30)

4 avocado slices

¼ cup Monterey Jack cheese, shredded

¼ cup tomatoes, diced

2 tablespoons sour cream

OPTIONAL ACCOMPANIMENT

¼ cup Pico de Gallo (page 36)

1 Preheat a 10-inch nonstick pan over medium-high heat.
2 When pan is hot, add crepe and immediately add eggs, ensuring complete coverage of the crepe.
3 Add ham, onions, mushrooms and avocado over the entire crepe to ensure some of each ingredient is in every bite. Sprinkle with cheese.
4 Crepe is done when it can slide freely in the pan.
5 Fold in half and top with diced tomatoes and sour cream. Serve with a side of Pico de Gallo.

KEY WEST CREPE EGGS

SERVES 1

1 Crepe (page 58)

¼ cup Whipped Eggs (page 21)

¼ cup cooked turkey, diced

2 tablespoons cooked bacon, diced into ½-inch pieces

4 avocado slices

¼ cup Monterey Jack cheese, shredded

¼ cup tomatoes, diced

2 tablespoons sour cream

OPTIONAL ACCOMPANIMENTS

¼ cup Pico de Gallo (page 36)

1 Preheat a 10-inch nonstick pan over medium-high heat.
2 When pan is hot, add crepe and immediately add eggs, ensuring complete coverage of the crepe.
3 Add turkey, bacon and avocado over the entire crepe to ensure some of each ingredient is in every bite. Sprinkle with cheese.
4 Crepe is done when it can slide freely in the pan.
5 Fold in half and top with diced tomatoes and sour cream. Serve with a side of Pico de Gallo.

CHICKICHANGA

We came up with the name for this dish to describe our playful take on a breakfast burrito. The tortilla shell is cooked in butter, allowing the shell to brown and giving the impression that the dish has been fried. We add spicy chicken, chorizo, avocado and our Vera Cruz sauce, which is a combination of Hollandaise Sauce and fresh Pico de Gallo.

SERVES 1

- 1 tablespoon butter
- 1 8-inch flour tortilla
- ¼ cup Whipped Eggs (page 21)
- 1½ ounces cooked Cajun chicken, sliced
- ¼ cup cooked chorizo, crumbled
- 1 tablespoon Roasted Onions, (page 31)
- 2 tablespoons diced green chilies
- 4 avocado slices
- 3 tablespoons cheddar jack cheese, shredded
- 2 tablespoons Pico de Gallo (page 36)
- 2 tablespoons Hollandaise Sauce (page 53)
- 2 tablespoons sour cream

1. In a 10-inch nonstick pan, heat butter over medium heat. Add tortilla and cook until it begins to lightly brown.
2. Place eggs, chicken, chorizo, onions, chilies and avocado slices evenly on top of tortilla. Top with cheese.
3. When eggs are cooked, slide the filled tortilla onto a plate, roll up tortilla into a burrito, and top with Pico de Gallo, Hollandaise Sauce and sour cream.

HUEVOS RANCHEROS TOSTADAS

This popular Mexican-style dish is a favorite of our guests for plenty of reasons. But mostly because, instead of the soft tortilla frequently used in huevos rancheros dishes, we use a light and crisp tostada shell that adds a pop of crunch. Ingredients in Mexican dishes are inherently fresh, which is why this fits perfectly on our menu.

SERVES 1

FOR CHIVE CREAM

2 cups sour cream

¼ cup milk

¼ cup chives, cut fine

FOR CHIPOTLE SLAW

4 cups red cabbage, thinly sliced

4 cups green cabbage, thinly sliced

2 cups black beans, cooked, strained and rinsed

1 cup red radish, shaved

1 cup pepitas (pumpkin seeds)

¼ cup cilantro, chiffonade

Citrus Chipotle Dressing (page 123)

FOR TOSTADAS

2 tablespoons cooked chorizo, crumbled

2 Sunny-Side Up Eggs (page 20)

1 tablespoon feta cheese

3 tablespoons Chive Cream (recipe above)

2 tostada shells

4 tablespoons Avocado Mash (page 69), divided

2 tablespoons salsa verde, warm

2 teaspoons cilantro, chiffonade

1 cup Chipotle Slaw (recipe above)

PREPARE CHIVE CREAM

1. Place all ingredients in a mixing bowl and whisk until thoroughly combined.
2. Store in an airtight container in the refrigerator.

PREPARE CHIPOTLE SLAW

1. Place all ingredients in a mixing bowl and toss to combine.
2. Set aside until ready to serve.

PREPARE TOSTADAS

1. Heat chorizo in a pan. Place on top of eggs, then top with feta cheese.
2. Meanwhile, place 2 tablespoons of Avocado Mash on top of each tostada shell and spread evenly. Place an egg with chorizo and feta on top of the Avocado Mash on each tostada.
3. Ladle salsa verde over the top of the eggs and then top with Chive Cream. Garnish with cilantro, and serve with Chipotle Slaw.

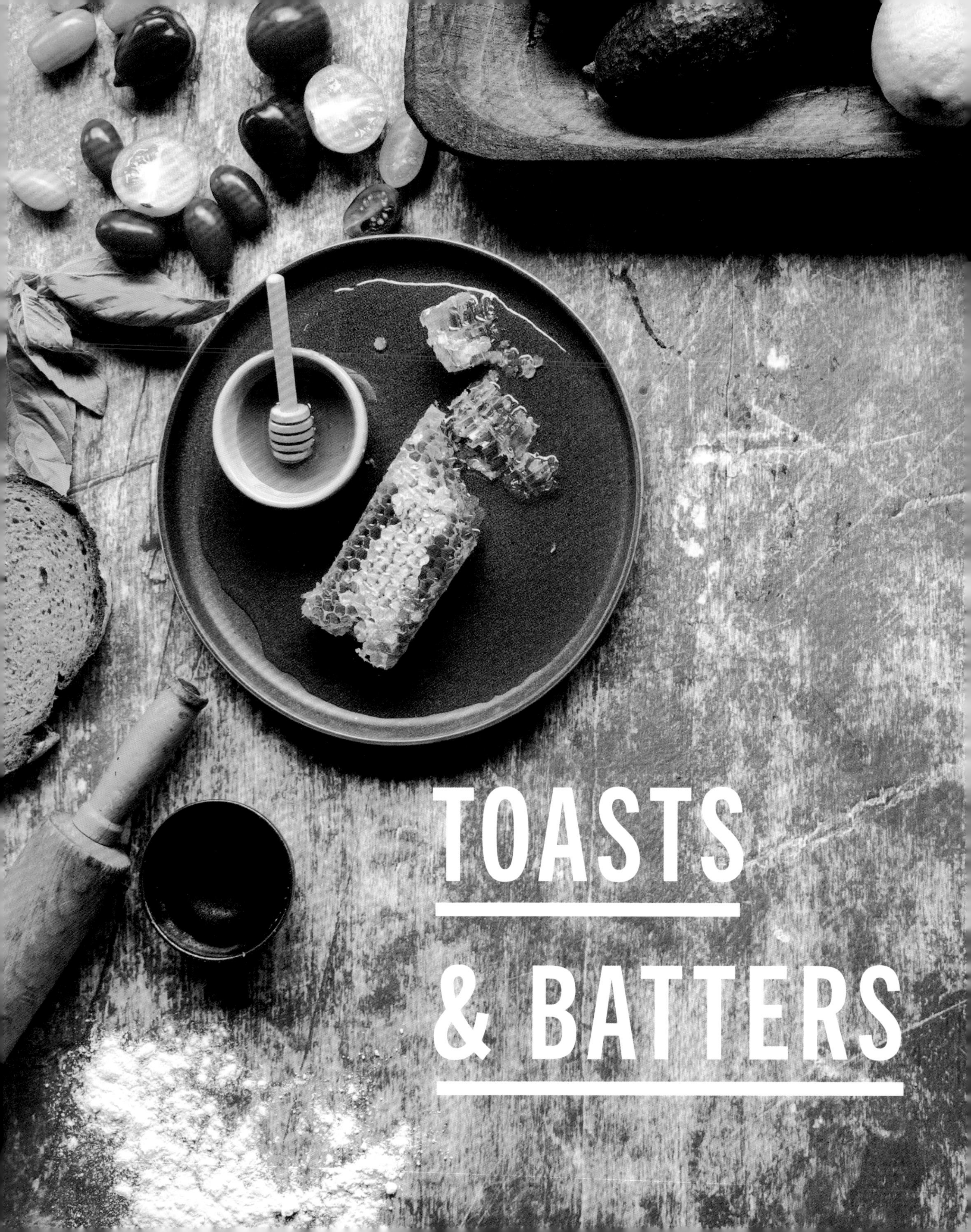

TOASTS & BATTERS

AVOCADO TOAST

We certainly didn't invent Avocado Toast, but we certainly did elevate it and were one of the first restaurant groups to put it on our menus. We use a whopping one and a half avocados on each order of our toast and keep them big, chunky and pure. Fresh lemon juice adds a ton of brightness to each bite and our thick-sliced, whole-grain artisan bread is the perfect bed on which it all rests. When you see this recipe, you'll notice the list of ingredients is very short. And we'd have it no other way.

SERVES 1

FOR AVOCADO MASH

3 avocados (about ¾ pound), halved, peeled and pitted

1 tablespoon fresh lemon juice

½ teaspoon First Watch Seasoning (page 26)

FOR AVOCADO TOAST

1 thick slice whole-grain artisan bread

2 eggs

¾ cups Avocado Mash (recipe above)

½ teaspoon extra-virgin olive oil (a fine-tip plastic squeeze bottle works best)

Pinch of Maldon sea salt

1 lemon wedge, for garnish

Freshly chopped parsley, for garnish

Freshly chopped chives, for garnish

PREPARE AVOCADO MASH

1. In a mixing bowl, combine avocados with lemon juice and seasoning until evenly coated.
2. Mash with a rubber spatula (or whisk), keeping medium-sized chunks. Don't over mash!
3. Transfer to an airtight container. Seal tightly with a double layer of plastic wrap pressed down directly onto the Avocado Mash to limit exposure to the air, which increases browning.
4. Keep in the refrigerator for at least 2 hours prior to serving, to ensure optimum temperature.

PREPARE AVOCADO TOAST

1. Toast 1 slice of bread.
2. Cook eggs, any style.
3. As eggs are cooking, spread toast evenly with Avocado Mash, retaining a rustic and chunky layer.
4. Slice toast in half and drizzle Avocado Mash with olive oil and sprinkle with Maldon sea salt.
5. Serve on a plate with eggs and a lemon wedge.
6. Garnish Avocado Toast and eggs with fresh herbs and serve immediately.

– NOTE –

Use your favorite "house" seasoning blend—ours has kosher salt, black pepper, garlic powder, onion salt and paprika but feel free to get creative!

RAINBOW TOAST

Once we got into the toast world with our Avocado Toast (page 69), we wanted to create another, sweeter version. Out of all our fresh, crisp fruit that we have in our kitchens, the Rainbow Toast was born. We start with thick and rich brioche bread, spread it with whipped ricotta cheese and then top it with a colorful array of the season's best fruit. It's such a beautiful dish and screams summer. Another cool fact is we drizzle the toast with local honey, sourced no farther than 100 miles from the restaurant you're dining in. It's kind of like an acceptable dessert for breakfast.

SERVES 1

- 1 piece brioche bread, sliced thick
- 3 tablespoons whipped ricotta cheese
- ¼ cup fresh strawberries, quartered
- ¼ cup fresh mango, diced
- ¼ cup fresh blackberries and blueberries
- 2 tablespoons First Watch Granola (page 33)
- Local honey

1. Toast brioche.
2. Slice toast vertically into 3 pieces and spread evenly with whipped ricotta.
3. Place toast on the center of a plate, making sure to retain shape.
4. Using a spoon, carefully lay strawberries in a horizontal line across the top of the toast.
5. Repeat with the diced mango, below the strawberries, and then with the blackberries and blueberries below the mango.
6. Sprinkle granola over the top of the toast, then drizzle evenly with honey and serve immediately.

FLORIDIAN FRENCH TOAST

Since Florida is all about sunshine and fresh fruit, this French toast just says "Florida on a Plate" to us. To combat the sometimes-mushy consistency of this breakfast favorite, we spread sweet wheat germ on one side of the toast and sear it, which creates a deliciously crunchy crust. Top it with loads of fresh fruit, pure maple syrup and indulge in every sunny bite.

SERVES 1

FOR FIRST WATCH FRENCH TOAST BATTER

4 cups Whipped Eggs (page 21)

1½ cups half & half

3 tablespoons brown sugar

1 tablespoon vanilla extract

½ teaspoon cinnamon

FOR FLORIDAN FRENCH TOAST

½ cup First Watch French Toast Batter (recipe above)

2 thick slices brioche bread

¼ cup wheat germ

1 banana, sliced ¼ inch thick

3 strawberries, quartered

1 kiwi, peeled and sliced ¼ inch thick

Powdered cinnamon sugar

ACCOMPANIMENTS

¼ cup berry compote

Warm syrup

PREPARE FIRST WATCH FRENCH TOAST BATTER

1. In a medium-size mixing bowl, combine the sugar, vanilla and cinnamon, and blend with a whisk.
2. Add eggs and half & half.
3. Mix thoroughly with wire whisk.
4. Store in an airtight container in the refrigerator.

PREPARE FLORIDIAN FRENCH TOAST

1. Pour French toast batter into a pie plate. Set aside.
2. Preheat a nonstick 10-inch pan or griddle over medium to medium-high heat.
3. Dip bread in French toast batter to cover both sides.
4. Transfer bread to griddle. Sprinkle wheat germ on top of bread and cook for 2 minutes.
5. Flip bread and continue cooking until golden brown, about 3 more minutes.
6. Shingle French toast onto a plate, wheat germ side up, and top with fruit and powdered sugar.
7. Serve with a side of berry compote and warm syrup.

– NOTE –

A shortcut to making compote is to use pie filling or your favorite preserves (warmed slightly).

HEIRLOOM TOMATO & BURRATA TOAST

FOR MARINATED CHERRY TOMATOES

1 cup Lemon White Balsamic Vinaigrette (page 26)

¼ cup fresh basil, torn (by hand) into nickel-size pieces

1 quart heirloom cherry tomatoes, halved

FOR TOAST

1 thick slice whole-grain artisan bread

½ cup Marinated Cherry Tomatoes (recipe above)

2 ounces Burrata cheese

1 teaspoon extra-virgin olive oil (a fine-tip plastic squeeze bottle works best)

¼ teaspoon Maldon sea salt

2 Basted Eggs (page 19)

1 teaspoon Parmesan cheese, shredded

Freshly chopped parsley, for garnish

Freshly chopped chives, for garnish

Let's be honest—burrata is just the best. With the creamy texture of this soft cheese, we thought it perfect to put it on a piece of our crunchy whole-grain artisan toast and surround it with bursts of marinated cherry tomatoes. No two toasts will look the same, as our tomatoes are straight from the farm and come in all different shapes, sizes and colors.

SERVES 1

PREPARE MARINATED CHERRY TOMATOES

1. Whisk vinaigrette and basil in a mixing bowl.
2. Add tomatoes and toss to combine.
3. Transfer to an airtight container and refrigerate.

PREPARE TOAST

1. Toast bread.
2. On a large plate, top toasted bread with marinated tomatoes.
3. Add Burrata cheese to center of toast.
4. Drizzle toast with olive oil; sprinkle evenly with Maldon sea salt.
5. Serve with eggs on the side. Garnish eggs with Parmesan cheese and the entire dish with fresh herbs.

SMOKED SALMON TZATZIKI TOAST

This is a complete breakfast all at your fingertips. We use only the highest quality wild Alaska smoked sockeye salmon and pair it with loads of Mediterranean flavors—salty feta cheese, aromatic dill and savory Tzatziki cream cheese. Fair warning—you'll likely want to double the recipe for cream cheese, so you can save some for a quick weekday bagel or sandwich spread. It's that addictive.

SERVES 1

FOR TZATZIKI CREAM CHEESE

2 cups whipped cream cheese

2 tablespoons English cucumber, diced into ¼-inch cubes

2 tablespoons freshly chopped dill

1 tablespoon freshly chopped parsley

1 tablespoon freshly chopped chives

1 tablespoon lemon juice

1 teaspoon kosher salt

FOR SMOKED SALMON TZATZIKI TOAST

1 slice whole-grain artisan bread

1 tablespoon Tzatziki Cream Cheese (recipe above)

8 thin slices English cucumber

2 ounces Smoked Salmon (page 49), thinly sliced

8 paper-thin radish slices

8 pieces red onion, julienned

1 tablespoon feta cheese, crumbled

2 teaspoons fresh dill

2 Basted Eggs (page 19)

Freshly chopped parsley, for garnish

Freshly chopped chives, for garnish

PREPARE TZATZIKI CREAM CHEESE

1. In a mixing bowl, combine all ingredients using a rubber spatula until evenly incorporated.
2. Transfer to an airtight container and refrigerate.

PREPARE SMOKED SALMON TZATZIKI TOAST

1. Toast bread.
2. Evenly spread Tzatziki Cream Cheese over entire surface of toast, using the back of a soup spoon.
3. Carefully place cucumber slices evenly across the top of the cream cheese.
4. Place Smoked Salmon on top of cucumber slices.
5. Place radish and red onion over salmon.
6. Top with crumbled feta and dill. Serve with eggs topped with fresh herbs.

FIRST WATCH PANCAKES

When you read our menu at First Watch, be sure to heed our warning: these beauties are huge! We perfected our pancake batter so that each pancake is super light and fluffy, has tons of flavor and really rises up when cooked. They're the perfect texture. It's a combination of technical baking and lots of taste testing, which we happily obliged in. While we think our pancakes are flawless just the way they are, we also have lots of fun, delicious variations to satisfy every craving: think cheddar and bacon, lemon ricotta and carrot cake, to name a few.

MULTIGRAIN PANCAKE BATTER

MAKES 6 PANCAKES

- 2 cups all-purpose flour
- ½ cup granulated sugar
- 1 teaspoon baking soda
- 2 tablespoons baking powder
- ¼ cup rolled oats
- 1½ teaspoons cornmeal
- 1½ teaspoons flax seeds
- 1 teaspoon sesame seeds
- 3 eggs, whipped
- ½ cup half & half
- ½ cup evaporated milk
- ¼ cup water
- ½ cup butter, melted and cooled to room temperature

1. In a medium bowl, whisk together flour, sugar, baking soda, baking powder, oats, cornmeal, flax seeds and sesame seeds until blended.
2. In a separate, large mixing bowl, whisk together eggs, half & half, evaporated milk and water until blended.
3. Slowly pour dry ingredients into wet ingredients while whisking constantly. Batter will be thick.
4. Add melted, room temperature butter last, whisking until ingredients are thoroughly combined.
5. Pour about ¼ cup batter per pancake onto a 375°F (medium heat) preheated griddle.
6. Cook for about 1 to 1½ minutes per side, or until done. Turn once using the Around the World method (page 80).

BANANA GRANOLA CRUNCH

- ½ cup Multigrain Pancake Batter (page 79)
- ¼ banana, sliced ⅛ inch thick
- ¼ cup First Watch Granola (page 33)

Follow directions for Multigrain Pancake Batter, adding banana and granola shortly after ladling pancake batter onto the griddle.

AROUND THE WORLD

Created in the early days of First Watch, this method of flipping pancakes involves using the edge of a spatula to carefully loosen the edges of the pancake before flipping, by slowly moving all around the pancake to ensure it does not stick.

BLUEBERRY

- ½ cup Multigrain Pancake Batter (page 79)
- ¼ cup blueberries

Follow directions for Multigrain Pancake Batter, adding blueberries shortly after ladling pancake batter onto the griddle.

CHEDDAR & BACON

- ½ cup Multigrain Pancake Batter (page 79)
- ¼ cup cheddar cheese, shredded
- ¼ cup crispy bacon, diced

Follow directions for Multigrain Pancake Batter, adding cheddar cheese first, then bacon, shortly after ladling pancake batter onto the griddle.

CARROT CAKE

- ½ cup Multigrain Pancake Batter (page 79)
- ¼ cup Carrot Cake Mix (recipe at right)
- 1 tablespoon wheat germ
- Powdered cinnamon sugar

1. Follow directions for Multigrain Pancake Batter, adding carrot cake mix and wheat germ shortly after ladling pancake batter onto the griddle.
2. Garnish with powdered sugar.

CARROT CAKE MIX

MAKES ABOUT ¾ CUP

- ½ cup shredded carrots
- ¼ cup raisins
- ⅛ cup chopped pecans
- 1 teaspoon pumpkin pie spice

1. Combine all ingredients in a mixing bowl and whisk until thoroughly incorporated.
2. Transfer to an airtight container and refrigerate until ready to use.

LEMON RICOTTA

- 1 cup Multigrain Pancake Batter (page 79), divided
- ½ cup Ricotta Cream (recipe at right)
- 3 tablespoons lemon curd
- ½ cup strawberries, quartered
- Powdered cinnamon sugar

1. Follow directions to make Multigrain Pancake Batter. After ladling batter onto the griddle, swirl in Ricotta Cream (a large-tip plastic squeeze bottle works best).
2. Garnish with lemon curd and strawberries, and sprinkle with powdered sugar.

A shortcut to making true lemon curd, which is very labor intensive and requires a fair amount of skill, would be to combine equal parts lemon pie filling and whipped cream. Fold these 2 ingredients together just until the whipped cream is absorbed into the pie filling and you cannot see any white streaks.

RICOTTA CREAM

MAKES 1½ CUPS

- 1½ cups ricotta cheese
- Zest of 3 lemons

1. Combine all ingredients in a mixing bowl and whisk until thoroughly incorporated.
2. Transfer to an airtight container and refrigerate until ready to use.

LEMON BLUEBERRY QUINOA PANCAKES

¾ cup Multigrain Pancake Batter (page 79)

¼ cup frozen blueberries

3 tablespoons cooked quinoa

2 tablespoons Blueberry Lemon Butter (recipe below)

¼ cup First Watch Granola (page 33)

¼ cup mixed berry compote

Sprinkle of powdered cinnamon sugar

We set our sights on coming up with a healthier pancake, so our diners could indulge in pancakes to their heart's content. For our Lemon Blueberry Quinoa Pancakes, we start with our multigrain batter, ladle it onto a griddle and then add cooked quinoa and blueberries before flipping the pancake. Not only does this add balanced nutrition and an earthy nutty flavor, it also sears the quinoa on one side, creating a delicious crunch. Top it with Blueberry Lemon Butter and call it a perfect morning.

MAKES 3 PANCAKES

1 Ladle three ¼-cup pancake batter circles onto a heated griddle.
2 Add blueberries and quinoa, ensuring a bite of each in every bite of pancake.
3 When pancakes bubble and edges appear cooked, flip using the Around the World technique (page 80).
4 When second side is cooked, flip back and transfer pancakes to a plate.
5 Add 2 scoops of Blueberry Lemon Butter on top of each pancake.
6 Sprinkle granola over pancakes and top with powdered sugar.
7 Serve with mixed berry compote on the side.

– NOTE –

A shortcut to making compote is to use pie filling or your favorite preserves (warmed slightly).

BLUEBERRY LEMON BUTTER

MAKES 1½ CUPS

½ pound whipped butter, at room temperature

Zest of 3 lemons, minced

2 tablespoons powdered cinnamon sugar

½ cup frozen blueberries, thawed

1 Combine all ingredients in a mixing bowl and whisk until thoroughly incorporated.
2 Transfer to an airtight container and refrigerate until ready to use.

PUMPKIN PANCAKES

Our guests start begging us to roll out our fall Pumpkin Pancakes earlier and earlier each year. The pumpkin spice craze is unbelievable! But for good reason—these pancakes are worth the mouth-watering wait. We use canned pumpkin puree and pumpkin pie spice. Not overly sweet, they're like a warm hug from the inside.

MAKES ABOUT 6 PANCAKES

1 cup canned pumpkin puree

1 tablespoon pumpkin pie spice

1 batch (about 1 quart) Multigrain Pancake Batter (page 79)

ACCOMPANIMENTS

Whipped butter

Warm syrup

1. Combine pumpkin puree and pumpkin pie spice in a large stainless bowl. Mix well with a wire whisk until evenly incorporated.
2. Fold in Multigrain Pancake Batter.
3. Ladle about ¼ cup pancake batter onto a heated griddle.
4. When cake bubbles and edges appear cooked, flip using the Around the World technique (page 80).
5. When second side is cooked, flip back and serve with a scoop of whipped butter and warm syrup.

– NOTE –

Almost always, we choose fresh over canned, but in this case, the texture and flavor you get from canned pumpkin puree is second to none. But you'll want to stock up during the fall season when it is plentiful on grocery store shelves.

SUPERSEED PROTEIN PANCAKES

FOR ALMOND BUTTER SAUCE

½ cup almond butter

¼ cup hot water

¼ cup pancake syrup

FOR SUPERSEED CRUNCH

½ cup kasha

½ cup chia seeds

½ cup flax seeds

½ cup roasted sunflower seeds

FOR SUPERSEED PROTEIN PANCAKES

1 quart Multigrain Pancake Batter (page 79)

½ cup cottage cheese

½ cup rolled oats

4 tablespoons Superseed Crunch (recipe above), plus extra for garnish

¼ cup Almond Butter Sauce (recipe above)

¼ cup mixed berry compote

2 tablespoons fresh blueberries

¼ banana, sliced

– NOTE –

Superseed Crunch is a great addition to yogurt, fruit or salad as well!

Sure, pancakes and healthy are not two words that normally fit in one sentence, but in this case, we prove it can happen. We fold cottage cheese and rolled oats straight into our Multigrain Pancake Batter (page 79), then sprinkle a blend of kasha (roasted buckwheat), chia seeds, flax seeds and sunflower seeds on one side of the pancake before flipping. Drizzle our Almond Butter Sauce over a stack of these sizzling hot cakes and indulge, guilt free-ish.

MAKES 4 PANCAKES

PREPARE ALMOND BUTTER SAUCE

Mix ingredients in a bowl. Store in a squeeze bottle until ready to serve.

PREPARE SUPERSEED CRUNCH

1 Combine all ingredients in a mixing bowl and mix thoroughly.
2 Store in a cool, dry place until ready to use.

PREPARE SUPERSEED PROTEIN PANCAKES

1 Combine pancake batter, cottage cheese and oats in a large bowl, folding together using a rubber spatula until fully incorporated.
2 Ladle ¼ cup batter per pancake onto a heated griddle and sprinkle about 1 tablespoon of Superseed Crunch mixture into each pancake before flipping.
3 Finish cooking pancakes and top with Almond Butter Sauce, mixed berry compote, blueberries, bananas and finish with a spoonful of Superseed Crunch.

HANDHELDS & SANDWICHES

ELEVATED EGG SANDWICH

This sandwich has the best of everything and is true to its name. We use full-butter brioche bread, cage-free over-easy eggs and top it with the best Wisconsin Gruyère cheese. But what really takes it to the next level—we load it with a mound of our fresh Avocado Mash (page 69), drizzle peppery arugula with our Lemon White Balsamic Vinaigrette (page 26) and pile on crispy, salty bacon.

SERVES 1

- 1 teaspoon whipped butter
- 1 brioche bun
- 1 Over-Easy Egg (page 18)
- 1 slice Gruyère cheese
- 1 tablespoon mayonnaise
- 2 slices crispy bacon
- 2 tablespoons Avocado Mash (page 69)
- ½ cup arugula
- 1 tablespoon Lemon White Balsamic Vinaigrette (page 26)

1. Preheat broiler (if desired).
2. Butter the bottom brioche bun only and place it butter-side down in a nonstick 8-inch pan or griddle to brown, about 2 minutes.
3. In a separate nonstick 8-inch pan, top Over-Easy Egg with cheese. Place under broiler (if desired) to help melt the cheese.
4. Spread mayonnaise on the bottom bun and build the sandwich by adding the bacon in an X and top with the cheesy egg.
5. Spread Avocado Mash on the top bun. In small bowl, combine arugula and vinaigrette. Place lemon-dressed arugula on top of egg, place the top of the bun on the sandwich.

FARMER'S BISCUIT BREAKFAST SANDWICH

We know it's a hard decision to choose bacon or sausage. So, when your cravings scream sausage, this is the option for you. We sandwich all-natural pork sausage between a flaky, buttery biscuit and add sharp cheddar cheese, a yummy runny egg and fresh arugula. But the secret ingredient? Apple butter, and plenty of it.

SERVES 1

- 1 large buttermilk biscuit
- 1 teaspoon whipped butter
- 1 (2-ounce) all-natural pork sausage patty
- 1 Over-Easy Egg (page 18)
- 1 slice sharp cheddar cheese
- ½ tablespoon mayonnaise
- 1 tablespoon apple butter
- ¼ cup arugula
- 1 tablespoon Lemon White Balsamic Vinaigrette (page 26)

1. Preheat broiler (if desired).
2. Slice biscuit in half, butter the cut side and grill, cut-side down, in a nonstick pan or griddle for 2 to 3 minutes, until golden brown.
3. Sear sausage patty in a nonstick pan, about 2 minutes on each side.
4. In a separate nonstick 8-inch pan, top egg with cheese. Place under broiler (if desired) to help melt the cheese.
5. Evenly spread mayonnaise on the bottom half of the toasted biscuit. Spread apple butter on the top half of the biscuit.
6. Place sausage patty on the bottom of the biscuit, then place egg, with cheese, on top of the sausage patty.
7. In small bowl, combine arugula and vinaigrette. Carefully place lemon-dressed arugula on top of cheese and finish with the top biscuit.

FIRST WATCH BLTE

Simple, quality ingredients are what make our BLTE sandwich. For the 'B' we use thick-sliced hardwood smoked bacon; the 'L' is organic spring lettuce mix; the 'T' is a beefy, thick-sliced tomato; and finally, the 'E' is for two over-hard, cage-free eggs cooked to perfection. This sandwich has been a crowd favorite since our doors opened.

SERVES 1

2 tablespoons mayonnaise

2 slices whole-grain artisan bread

3 slices crispy bacon

2 Over Hard Eggs (page 19)

2 slices Monterey Jack cheese

2 slices tomato

1 cup spring mix

ACCOMPANIMENT

Lemon White Balsamic Vinaigrette Dressed Greens (page 26)

1. Spread mayonnaise evenly on each slice of bread.
2. Place bacon on one slice of bread; top with eggs and 1 slice of cheese on top of the eggs.
3. On the other slice of bread, place tomato slices and the other slice of cheese on top of the tomato.
4. Add spring mix to the bacon-egg side, then close the sandwich.
5. Serve with lemon-dressed greens.

MARKET VEGGIE

We wanted to make a sandwich that showcased our fresh, house-roasted vegetables, and this Market Veggie was the solution. We use a bright, basil pesto to hold everything together and sear the bread like you're making a grilled cheese to add a crunchy texture. It's hearty, refreshing and flavorful.

SERVES 1

- 1 tablespoon whipped butter
- 2 slices whole-grain artisan bread
- 1 tablespoon mayonnaise
- ¼ cup Roasted Zucchini (page 31)
- ¼ cup Roasted Crimini Mushrooms (page 30)
- 1 tablespoon basil pesto
- 1 cup spinach leaves
- 2 tablespoons mozzarella cheese, shredded

1. Preheat broiler.
2. Butter both slices of bread and place them in a nonstick pan or griddle, butter side down. Grill for about 2 minutes, or until golden brown.
3. Spread mayonnaise on one slice of bread, then layer on zucchini and mushrooms.
4. On the other slice of bread, spread pesto and then layer spinach and mozzarella.
5. Place the sandwich under the broiler, open faced, to melt the mozzarella and warm the vegetables.
6. Remove from the broiler and close the sandwich.
7. To serve, cut in half.

POWER WRAP

Our Power Wrap is an egg white frittata rolled up in a tortilla. Think of it as a convenient, handheld way to eat breakfast, perfect for those mornings when you're rushing out the door to a meeting or trying to get the kids to school on time. It also stays neat and tidy since everything is cooked into the frittata. We use nonstick cooking spray instead of butter to keep it light and healthy.

SERVES 1

- Nonstick cooking spray
- ¾ cup egg whites
- ½ cup spinach leaves
- 2 tablespoons cooked turkey, diced
- 2 tablespoons Roasted Crimini Mushrooms (page 30)
- 1 tablespoon mozzarella cheese, shredded
- 1 (10-inch) flour tortilla
- ¼ cup Pico de Gallo (page 36)

1. Lightly spray a nonstick 10-inch pan with cooking spray and heat over medium heat. Add egg whites.
2. Add spinach, turkey and mushrooms, and cook the frittata until completely set.
3. Once set, sprinkle with cheese, then lay tortilla on top.
4. Turn pan upside down on a cutting board, so the tortilla is on the bottom. Roll up the wrap and cut straight in half.
5. Serve with a side of Pico de Gallo.

ROAST BEEF & HAVARTI

This beefy masterpiece is kind of like an inside-out grilled cheese. Searing Parmesan on the outside of the sourdough bread creates a wonderfully crunchy texture and adds a nutty flavor to each bite. And that's just the bread. Inside we load this sandwich with roast beef, roasted vegetables, peppery arugula and creamy Havarti. Serve with your favorite horseradish sauce for extra spice.

SERVES 1

2 slices Parmesan-Crusted Sourdough bread

2 slices horseradish Havarti cheese

4½ ounces roast beef, thinly shaved

¼ cup Roasted Tomatoes (page 32)

¼ cup Roasted Onions (page 31)

½ cup arugula

1 tablespoon Lemon White Balsamic Vinaigrette (page 26)

Horseradish sauce

1. Heat 2 slices of Parmesan-Crusted Sourdough, cheese side down, over medium heat in a 10-inch nonstick pan or griddle.
2. While the bread heats, place 1 slice of Havarti on a slice of bread. Top with roast beef.
3. On the other slice of bread, place 1 slice of Havarti, then the roasted tomatoes and onions.
4. Once all cheese is fully melted, remove each half from the pan. In small bowl, combine arugula and vinaigrette. Add lemon-dressed arugula to the roast beef side, and then close the sandwich.
5. Cut in half and serve with a side of horseradish sauce.

PARMESAN-CRUSTED SOURDOUGH

Spread 1 tablespoon whipped butter on one side of a slice of sourdough bread. Sprinkle with shredded Parmesan cheese until evenly coated.

HAM & GRUYÈRE MELT

Ham and cheese is a classic sandwich combination, but this version will quickly become your favorite. We use Grand Cru Gruyère cheese from Wisconsin. It has a nutty flavor profile that pairs perfectly with the salty ham. To really impress your guests, turn this sandwich into a Croque Madame.

SERVES 1

- 1 tablespoon whipped butter
- 2 slices brioche bread
- 4½ ounces cooked ham, thinly shaved
- 2 tablespoons Dijonnaise (equal parts Dijon mustard and mayonnaise)
- 2 slices Gruyère cheese
- 2 slices tomato

1. Preheat broiler.
2. Butter both pieces of brioche and place in a nonstick 10-inch pan or onto a griddle over medium heat, butter side down.
3. Place ham in a nonstick 8-inch pan or griddle over medium heat and cook for 1 minute; flip and cook for another minute to heat through.
4. Spread Dijonnaise evenly over the non-buttered sides of both slices of bread.
5. Place warm ham on one slice of bread and top with one slice of cheese. Place tomato slices on the other slice of bread along with the other slice of cheese. Place the sandwich under the broiler, open-faced, to melt cheese. Once cheese is bubbling, remove from broiler and close the sandwich.
6. To serve, cut in half.

CROQUE MADAME

Top with ½ cup of béchamel sauce and 2 eggs cooked to desired doneness. This makes a huge sandwich, so a fork and knife are recommended.

CHICKEN SALAD

1 pound cooked chicken breast, cut into bite-sized pieces

½ cup water chestnuts, drained and diced

½ cup raisins

¾ cup celery, diced small

⅓ cup mayonnaise

⅓ cup Fuji apples, diced small

We make our chicken salad fresh in-house and use seasoned, roasted chicken, but feel free to use grilled or pan-seared. Our recipe for chicken salad has remained relatively constant since our first restaurant opened in the '80s, but we love to change it up with these fruity and cheesy variations.

SERVES 1

1 Place all ingredients in a mixing bowl.
2 Using a rubber spatula, mix ingredients together until thoroughly blended.

FRUITY CHICKEN

1 cup spinach leaves

1 slice tomato

¾ cup Chicken Salad (recipe above)

2 cups fresh mixed fruit

¼ cup Poppy Seed Dressing (page 125)

1 Cover two-thirds of a plate with loose spinach leaves.
2 In the center, place a tomato slice.
3 Place a scoop of chicken salad on the tomato slice.
4 Evenly spread the 2 cups of fresh fruit on the bed of spinach leaves.
5 Serve with dressing on the side.

CHICKEN SALAD MELT

- 1 teaspoon whipped butter
- 1 slice whole-grain artisan bread
- ½ cup Chicken Salad (page 104)
- 2 slices tomato
- 1 slice Monterey Jack cheese
- Freshly chopped parsley, for garnish
- Freshly chopped chives, for garnish

1. Place oven rack in the middle position and preheat broiler.
2. Butter the artisan bread and grill in an 8-inch nonstick pan or electric griddle. Top with chicken salad.
3. Top chicken salad with tomato slices and cheese.
4. Place under the broiler, on a cookie sheet, until cheese is melted and starting to turn slightly brown.
5. Carefully remove from broiler and sprinkle with fresh herbs to serve.

BOWLS & SALADS

SUNRISE GRANOLA BOWL

Before açaí bowls and chia seed pudding, there was this dish—the quintessential yogurt fruit parfait. This classic has been on the menu, under different names, since the start. We once called it the Siesta Key Cocktail, which paid homage to First Watch's headquarters in Sarasota, on Florida's Gulf coast. We've amped it up just a touch and now use Greek yogurt to add more protein. You can eat this granola bowl every day and never get tired of it.

SERVES 1

½ cup First Watch Granola (page 33)

⅔ cup vanilla Greek yogurt, divided

16 pieces fresh fruit, mixed, divided

Sprinkle of powdered cinnamon sugar

1 Place ¼ cup granola in a bowl.
2 Add ⅓ cup yogurt.
3 Add 4 pieces of fresh fruit.
4 Add ⅓ cup yogurt.
5 Add ¼ cup granola.
6 Top with 12 pieces of fresh fruit and finish with powdered cinnamon sugar.
7 Serve on a plate with a fresh-baked muffin and a large spoon.

– NOTE –

At First Watch, we use whatever fruit is in season: strawberries, honeydew, pineapples, grapes, watermelon, bananas, kiwi. Use whatever you have handy and sweet.

A.M. SUPERFOODS BOWL

FOR CHIA SEED PUDDING
MAKES 3 CUPS

½ cup black chia seeds

1 teaspoon kosher salt

2 cups coconut milk, canned (culinary coconut milk, not the beverage)

¼ cup agave nectar

1 teaspoon vanilla extract

FOR SUPERFOODS BOWL

1 slice whole-grain artisan bread

¼ cup almond butter

¼ teaspoon Maldon sea salt

¾ cup Chia Seed Pudding (recipe above)

2 tablespoons blackberry preserves

½ banana, sliced ⅛ inch thick

2 strawberries, quartered (8 pieces)

¼ cup blueberries

¼ cup First Watch Granola (page 33)

– NOTE –

Maldon sea salt is one of the finest salts in the world. We use it for its light, flaky texture and delicate flavor.

At First Watch, we try not to jump on trendy culinary bandwagons. But after chia seeds started popping up everywhere and in everything, we gave this powerhouse seed a close look and found it fit perfectly with our food mission. Chia seeds contain lots of healthy omega-3 fatty acids, calcium, antioxidants and protein, but some people are put off by the texture. That's why we soak the seeds in full-fat coconut milk, giving the dish a creamy-pudding-like appeal. We top it with blackberry preserves, housemade granola and mounds of fresh fruit for the perfect balance.

SERVES 1

PREPARE CHIA SEED PUDDING

1 In a large mixing bowl, combine chia seeds and salt.
2 In a separate mixing bowl, combine coconut milk, agave and vanilla extract and mix with a whisk until all ingredients are incorporated.
3 Add liquid ingredients to the dry mixture and combine with a whisk until fully incorporated.
4 Transfer to a large, airtight container.
5 Cover and refrigerate for at least 2 hours (or overnight, if possible) before use to allow the chia to "bloom." Stirring may be required after 1 hour.

FINISH SUPERFOODS BOWL

1 Toast one slice of whole-grain artisan bread.
2 Cut toast corner to corner and spread with almond butter, using the back of a spoon. Sprinkle with Maldon sea salt.
3 Place a ¾-cup scoop of Chia Seed Pudding in a bowl.
4 Add blackberry preserves around the edge of the bowl, on top of the chia seed pudding.
5 Add sliced bananas, strawberries and blueberries.
6 Add granola on top of the fruit.
7 Serve with almond-buttered toast on the side.

BÁNH MÌ BREAKFAST BOWL

We're always looking for the next new thing at First Watch, and the Bánh Mì Breakfast Bowl was the answer. As bacon experts, this braised pork belly is right in our wheelhouse. We use a whole side of pork belly, cook it for 2 hours, slice it, add our Five-Spice Glaze (recipe below) and then crisp it in a sauté pan. This bowl explodes with flavor and will definitely jump-start your day. Jalapeños and Sriracha add a kick of spice, while the daikon and carrots add reprieve and crunch. We put soy sauce in the grains/rice, adding a richness to the overall flavor profile. It's the perfect brunch item.

SERVES 1

FOR BRAISED PORK BELLY BACON

2 cups carrots, cut into coins

1 cup onion, julienned

2 quarts chicken stock

6 to 7 pounds smoked pork belly (slab bacon)

FOR FIVE-SPICE GLAZE

1 cup Million Dollar Bacon Glaze (page 23)

1 tablespoon five-spice powder

FOR SOY MARINATED GRAINS BLEND

4 cups cooked grain blend (even parts brown rice, quinoa, farro)

2 tablespoons soy sauce

2 tablespoons water

PREPARE BRAISED PORK BELLY BACON

1. Preheat convection oven to 325°F.
2. Place carrots and onions into a 2-inch deep roasting pan.
3. Place whole pork belly, fat-side up, on top of carrots and onions.
4. Pour chicken stock into roasting pan.
5. Cover roasting pan with plastic wrap to seal tight, then cover tightly with aluminum foil.
6. Place roasting pan into oven and bake at 325°F for 2 hours.
7. Remove from oven, then remove foil and plastic wrap to cool to room temperature (about 1 hour).
8. Remove pork belly, wrap in plastic and refrigerate overnight.

PREPARE FIVE-SPICE GLAZE

1. In a mixing bowl, combine all ingredients using a whisk.
2. Transfer to a squeeze bottle with a medium tip.

PREPARE SOY MARINATED GRAINS BLEND

In a large mixing bowl, combine all ingredients. Stir with a rubber spatula until fully incorporated. Set aside until ready to use.

– RECIPE CONTINUES ON PAGE 114 –

BÁNH MÌ BREAKFAST BOWL

CONTINUED FROM PAGE 113

FOR DAIKON CARROT SLAW

1 cup rice wine vinegar

¼ cup granulated sugar

1 teaspoon kosher salt

2 cups daikon radish, julienned

1 cup shredded carrot

FOR BÁNH MÌ BREAKFAST BOWL

3 ounces Braised Pork Belly Bacon (page 113), diced

1 tablespoon Five-Spice Glaze (page 113)

2 Sunny-Side Up Eggs (page 20)

1 cup Soy Marinated Grains Blend (page 113)

7 thin slices fresh jalapeño

½ cup Daikon Carrot Slaw (recipe above)

Sriracha sauce

2 teaspoons cilantro, chiffonade

– NOTE –

We use smoked pork belly, or slab bacon, because it brings a wonderful depth of flavor to these recipes. Slab bacon can be purchased from your local butcher. The smoking process breaks down the meat allowing for a shorter cook time during the braising step.

PREPARE DAIKON CARROT SLAW

1. In a sauce pot, combine rice wine vinegar, sugar and salt. Bring to a boil.
2. While mixture is heating, wash the daikon radish thoroughly to remove any dirt and peel the outside of the daikon radish to remove outer surface.
3. Using a julienne peeler or Asian mandoline, peel the daikon radish to create julienne strips. Cut the julienned daikon strips to about 2-inches in length. Combine daikon and carrots in a large bowl and set aside.
4. Once the vinegar sauce is boiling, remove from heat and pour over daikon and carrots.
5. Cover and refrigerate for at least 4 hours before use.

FINISH BÁNH MÌ BREAKFAST BOWL

1. In a preheated egg pan, sear diced pork belly bacon until mahogany brown, about 5 minutes. Using a rubber spatula, strain off excess liquid and discard. Add Five-Spice Glaze; let glaze start to bubble and carefully swirl pan to coat pork belly.
2. In another pan, heat Soy Marinated Grains Blend for about 2 minutes.
3. Transfer grains to the center of a bowl.
4. At the 12 o'clock position of the bowl, place sliced jalapeño.
5. To the right of the jalapeño, place the Daikon Carrot Slaw.
6. Next to the slaw, place the pork belly.
7. Carefully lay Sunny-Side Up Eggs over the center/left edge so they lightly drape over the slaw and pork belly.
8. Make a thin zigzag line of Sriracha over the eggs.
9. Sprinkle cilantro over the entire dish.

POWER BREAKFAST QUINOA BOWL

The inspiration of this dish came from dozens of First Watch servers, who, after working at the restaurant for a long time and eating everything on the menu, started ordering a combination of a few different bowls. The aroma of this dish is fantastic and the flavors run deep with tons of roasted vegetables. Throw two eggs on top and you can imagine why the employees came up with this creative meal.

SERVES 1

½ cup cooked Italian sausage, crumbled

½ cup kale, cut into ½-inch strips

2 tablespoons Roasted Tomatoes (page 32)

2 tablespoons Roasted Crimini Mushrooms (page 30)

1 cup quinoa, cooked

¼ cup chicken stock

2 tablespoons Lemon White Balsamic Vinaigrette (page 26)

2 Basted Eggs (page 19)

1 teaspoon extra-virgin olive oil (a fine-tip plastic squeeze bottle works best)

½ tablespoon Parmesan cheese, shredded, for garnish

Freshly chopped parsley, for garnish

Freshly chopped chives, for garnish

1. Heat a 10-inch nonstick pan over medium-high heat. Add sausage, kale, tomatoes and mushrooms and sauté for 2 minutes.
2. Add quinoa and chicken stock and continue to cook until chicken stock has evaporated and kale is slightly wilted, about 3 minutes.
3. Add vinaigrette to quinoa mixture and toss to coat all ingredients evenly.
4. Transfer quinoa mixture to a salad bowl.
5. Place eggs on top.
6. Drizzle olive oil over eggs and garnish with Parmesan and fresh herbs.

PESTO CHICKEN QUINOA BOWL

FOR BASIL PESTO DRESSING

1 cup ranch dressing

½ cup basil pesto

FOR PESTO CHICKEN QUINOA BOWL

6 tablespoons chicken stock, divided

½ cup kale, cut into strips

2 tablespoons carrots, julienned

1 cup quinoa, cooked

4 ounces cooked chicken, cut into bite-sized pieces

2 tablespoons Lemon White Balsamic Vinaigrette (page 26)

1 tablespoon feta cheese, crumbled

1 tablespoon Roasted Tomatoes, (page 32)

2 tablespoons Basil Pesto Dressing (recipe above)

Freshly chopped parsley, for garnish

Freshly chopped chives, for garnish

2 fresh lemon wedges, for garnish (if desired)

We're proud to say that we've been serving quinoa since the days it was such a new menu item that no one knew how to pronounce it. Quinoa is an ancient grain and is a great carrier for big, bold flavors like pesto. This dish is so well balanced with the acidity of the vinaigrette, subtle creaminess of the quinoa and protein of the chicken. It even won us a Menu Masters Award, which is the highest award you can win in the restaurant industry. Call it an Oscar of our world.

SERVES 1

PREPARE BASIL PESTO DRESSING

1. In a mixing bowl, combine both ingredients thoroughly with a wire whisk.
2. Transfer to an airtight container and refrigerate.

FINISH PESTO CHICKEN QUINOA BOWL

1. In a 10-inch nonstick pan, combine 4 tablespoons chicken stock with kale and carrots. Top with cooked quinoa and sauté over medium-high heat for 3 minutes, until chicken stock has evaporated and kale starts to soften.
2. In an 8-inch nonstick pan, sauté chicken with 2 tablespoons chicken stock until stock has evaporated. In same pan, add vinaigrette to the heated chicken and top with feta cheese and roasted tomatoes. Keep warm without melting the feta (about 30 seconds).
3. Place quinoa mixture in a salad bowl. Add sautéed chicken, feta and tomatoes on top of the quinoa. Drizzle Basil Pesto Dressing over entire bowl. Garnish with fresh herbs and fresh lemon wedges (if desired).

SWEET HONEY CHICKEN PECAN SALAD

FOR HONEY DIJON MUSTARD DRESSING

¼ cup balsamic vinegar

1 tablespoon Dijon mustard

1 tablespoon honey

1 teaspoon kosher salt

Freshly ground black pepper, to taste

½ cup olive oil

FOR SALAD

3 ounces grilled chicken breast, sliced

2 tablespoons crispy bacon, ½-inch diced

¼ cup pecans

6 tablespoons Honey Dijon Mustard Dressing (recipe above)

2 cups romaine lettuce, chopped

2 cups spring mix

¼ cup fresh tomatoes, diced

2 tablespoons cheddar jack cheese, shredded

2 tablespoons carrots, julienned

4 slices avocado

1 ciabatta crisp, buttered

This salad offers a pleasant surprise—it's served warm. Well, partially. We warm the chicken, bacon and dressing together in a sauté pan and then pour it over the greens, which helps to gently wilt the greens below. Another surprise in this salad is an unexpected spicy flavor, which comes from the Dijon mustard in the dressing. Spice from Dijon mustard is like a wasabi spice—it hits you deep in the back of your nose and is just delicious.

SERVES 1

PREPARE HONEY DIJON MUSTARD DRESSING

1 Whisk first five ingredients in a bowl.
2 Slowly add oil while whisking.
3 Store in an airtight container and refrigerate.

FINISH SALAD

1 In an 8-inch nonstick pan, re-heat grilled chicken and bacon. Add pecans and Honey Dijon Mustard Dressing.
2 While ingredients are heating, combine romaine and spring mix in a salad bowl and top with tomatoes, cheese and carrots.
3 Arrange avocados in a ring around the center of the bowl, leaving space in the center for the hot ingredients.
4 Place hot ingredients on top of the salad in the center of the avocado ring, being careful not to cover avocados, and serve with ciabatta crisp.

– NOTE –

We serve our salads with a ciabatta crisp instead of croutons, but feel free to add your favorite croutons for crunch!

CHICKEN AVOCADO CHOP

Let's be honest—salads can be pretty boring. However, this one is anything but. We wanted to give our customers something fun and elevated, and we think this Southwest-inspired salad delivers. Chop salads are great because you get all the bite-sized ingredients on every forkful. With corn, black beans, avocado, tomatoes, tortilla strips and a sweet and spicy chipotle dressing, this quickly became one of our most popular dishes.

SERVES 1

FOR CITRUS CHIPOTLE DRESSING

½ cup orange juice

½ cup lime juice

3 teaspoons honey

1 clove garlic

4 chipotle chilies in adobo sauce, divided

½ cup extra-virgin olive oil

Salt and pepper to taste

FOR SALAD

2 cups romaine lettuce, chopped

2 cups arugula

3 ounces grilled chicken breast, sliced

2 tablespoons canned corn

2 tablespoons canned black beans, drained and rinsed

¼ cup feta cheese, crumbled

¼ cup Citrus Chipotle Dressing (recipe above)

2 tablespoons fresh tomatoes, diced

4 slices fresh avocado

½ cup tri-color tortilla strips

Freshly chopped parsley, for garnish

Freshly chopped chives, for garnish

PREPARE CITRUS CHIPOTLE DRESSING

1. In a food processor or blender, combine orange and lime juices, honey, garlic and 2 of the 4 chipotle peppers. Process and slowly (and we mean slowly, like a slow drizzle) add oil to incorporate. Taste and adjust to your liking by adding extra peppers and/or a dash of salt and pepper.
2. Store in an airtight container in the refrigerator. (Dressing is best if made a day ahead of time. If dressing separates, simply shake or stir to mix, just before use.)

FINISH SALAD

1. In a large mixing bowl, combine romaine, arugula, chicken, corn, beans and feta. Toss with dressing and transfer to a salad bowl.
2. Garnish with fresh diced tomatoes, avocado slices, tortilla strips and fresh herbs.

SALAD MARINADE

This nostalgic dish has been on our menu since our opening days in Pacific Grove, California, and pays homage to the beautiful produce that came from right around us. It's simple, delicious and bright and celebrates fresh ingredients. It speaks to our history and our original fresh-food philosophy that we still hold dear today.

SERVES 1

FOR POPPY SEED DRESSING

¾ cup white wine vinegar

½ cup lemon juice

2 cups sugar

1 tablespoon kosher salt

1 tablespoon dry mustard powder

1½ cups onions, diced

3 tablespoons poppy seeds

3 cups canola oil

½ cup sour cream

FOR SALAD

2 cups tomatoes, diced small

1 cup zucchini, diced small

1 cup celery, diced small

1 cup Poppy Seed Dressing (recipe above)

PREPARE POPPY SEED DRESSING

1. Mix all ingredients, except for canola oil and sour cream, with a wire whisk.
2. Slowly add oil in a stream, whisking to incorporate with the other ingredients.
3. Add sour cream and whisk until fully incorporated.
4. Transfer to an airtight container and refrigerate until ready to use.

FINISH SALAD

1. Measure tomatoes, celery and zucchini into a large mixing bowl.
2. Add 1 quart of well-mixed Poppy Seed Dressing to the vegetables. Mix thoroughly with a rubber spatula.
3. Serve as a side or on a bed of your favorite greens—we love arugula, but spinach or spring mix will work as well.

HASHES & SKILLETS

SHRIMP & GRITS

FOR CHEDDAR/PARMESAN CHEESE GRITS

4 cups water

½ tablespoon kosher salt

1 cup Bob's Red Mill® yellow corn grits

½ cup cheddar jack cheese, shredded

½ cup Parmesan cheese, shredded

1 teaspoon First Watch Seasoning (page 26)

FOR SHRIMP & GRITS

7 raw shrimp (26/30 or 21/25 size)

1 to 2 tablespoons blackened seasoning

1 tablespoon blended oil

¼ cup green bell pepper, diced small

¼ cup andouille sausage, diced

¼ cup Roasted Onions (page 31)

¼ cup Roasted/Charred Corn (page 132)

2 tablespoons Roasted Tomatoes (page 32)

¼ cup chicken stock

¾ cup Cheddar/Parmesan Cheese Grits (recipe above)

Freshly chopped parsley, for garnish

Freshly chopped chives, for garnish

We start with high-quality Bob's Red Mill® yellow corn grits and add a ton of Parmesan, cheddar and jack cheese. Fresh shrimp makes all the difference. Add in all the fixings, like roasted vegetables, blackened seasoning, spicy andouille sausage and this dish is everything you could ever need for brunch.

SERVES 1

PREPARE CHEDDAR/PARMESAN CHEESE GRITS

1. Bring water and salt to a boil.
2. Add grits and whisk continuously for 5 minutes.
3. After 5 minutes, whisk in cheeses and continue mixing until cheeses are fully incorporated.
4. Remove from heat and let rest for 5 minutes, then add First Watch seasoning and whisk until fully incorporated. Cover and keep warm until ready to serve.

FINISH SHRIMP & GRITS

1. Sprinkle shrimp liberally with blackened seasoning.
2. Heat oil in a 10-inch nonstick pan over medium heat. Add green pepper, shrimp and sausage and sauté for 60 seconds.
3. Add roasted onions, corn and roasted tomatoes to the pan and cook for an additional 60 seconds. Add chicken stock to deglaze the pan, and cook until half of the chicken stock has evaporated, about 30 seconds.
4. Plate grits in a mound in the middle of a bowl.
5. Pour contents of the pan onto the middle of the grits. Sprinkle fresh herbs over the top and serve.

PORK BELLY BACON & GRITS

As the breakfast experts, we are connoisseurs of bacon in all its delicious forms. For this bowl, we take whole smoked pork belly and braise it. Braising makes it super tender, like a juicy steak. Then we slice it into thick pieces and sear it, bringing out even more depth of flavor and texture. The only thing that could make this bacon better was a big bowl of cheesy grits and poached eggs, and that's our professional opinion.

SERVES 1

3 slices Braised Pork Belly Bacon (page 113), about 4 inches long, ¼ inch thick

¾ cup Cheddar/Parmesan Cheese Grits (page 129)

2 Poached Eggs (page 20)

2 shakes Cajun or blackened seasoning

2 tablespoons pickled peppers, sliced

Freshly chopped parsley, for garnish

Freshly chopped chives, for garnish

1. Sear braised bacon slices in a preheated 8-inch nonstick pan for 3 minutes per side.
2. Place cheese grits into a serving dish.
3. Place seared bacon on top of grits.
4. Place eggs in center of bacon slices and sprinkle Cajun seasoning on top.
5. Place peppers in a tall mound between the eggs.
6. Garnish the entire dish with fresh herbs.

ELOTE MEXICAN STREET CORN HASH

FOR ROASTED/CHARRED CORN

8 ears of corn, husked

¼ cup canola oil

½ tablespoon First Watch Seasoning (page 26)

FOR CHIPOTLE CREMA

1 cup sour cream

1 cup chipotle chilies in adobo sauce, pureed

¼ cup half & half

1 tablespoon lime juice

FOR ELOTE HASH

½ tablespoon butter

1½ cups First Watch Potatoes (page 24)

¼ cup Roasted/Charred Corn (recipe above)

2 tablespoons cooked chorizo, crumbled

2 tablespoons crumbled cotija cheese

2 tablespoons fresh cilantro, leaves only, chopped

¼ cup cheddar jack cheese, shredded

2 tablespoons green onions, sliced

2 eggs, cooked any style

1 tablespoon Chipotle Crema (recipe above)

3 slices avocado

ACCOMPANIMENTS

2 tortillas (corn or flour)

1 lime wedge

Elote is a popular Mexican corn dish typically sold at little roadside stands. We wanted to showcase this flavorful food, so we turned ours into a hash with crumbled chorizo, cotija cheese, cilantro, chipotle crema and fresh avocado. It's bursting with flavor and might win you over as your favorite item on our menu.

SERVES 1

PREPARE ROASTED/CHARRED CORN

1 Preheat oven to 400°F.
2 In a large mixing bowl or rimmed baking sheet, combine husked ears of corn, oil and seasoning and toss until corn is evenly coated.
3 Transfer corn to a roasting rack on a sheet pan, leaving space between the cobs to allow air circulation during cooking and cooling.
4 Bake for 15 minutes, rotate and cook an additional 15 minutes, until kernels are roasted with some dark/charred spots.
5 Remove from oven and let rest for 15 minutes. Then, using a sharp knife, carefully remove kernels and discard cobs.
6 Transfer to an airtight container and refrigerate until ready to serve.

PREPARE CHIPOTLE CREMA

1 Measure ingredients into a mixing bowl and whisk to combine.
2 Transfer to a plastic squeeze bottle and refrigerate until needed.

FINISH ELOTE HASH

1 Melt butter in an 8-inch nonstick pan. Add potatoes, corn and chorizo.
2 Sauté in the pan over medium heat until all ingredients are heated through, about 3 minutes.
3 In a small bowl, combine cotija cheese and cilantro. Once the hash is hot, top with shredded cheese, 2 tablespoons cotija/cilantro blend and green onions. Transfer to a plate.
4 Top with eggs and drizzle with Chipotle Crema.
5 Garnish with avocado and 1 tablespoon cotija/cilantro blend.
6 Heat tortillas for 15 seconds per side on the griddle.
7 Serve hash with warm tortillas and a lime wedge.

POT ROAST HASH

You've heard of breakfast for dinner, but this is our twist on dinner for breakfast. Save your leftover pot roast and make this hearty hash the next morning. We add red and yellow bell peppers, sweet shallots and a demi-glace sauce for an even deeper, richer flavor. It's such a perfect way to start your day that you might forget pot roast ever went with dinner.

SERVES 1

½ tablespoon butter

½ cup fully cooked pot roast, cut in bite-sized pieces (leftovers work perfectly)

2 tablespoons roasted bell peppers, drained and diced

2 tablespoons Roasted Shallots (page 32)

1½ cups First Watch Potatoes (page 24)

¼ cup demi-glace sauce

2 eggs, cooked any style

Freshly chopped parsley, for garnish

Freshly chopped chives, for garnish

1 Melt butter in a 10-inch nonstick pan. Add pot roast, roasted peppers, shallots and potatoes.

2 Sauté in the pan, over medium heat, until all ingredients are heated throughout, about 3 minutes.

3 Once hot, add demi-glace sauce to pan and heat for 30 more seconds.

4 Once sauce is bubbling, transfer to a plate.

5 Top with eggs and fresh herbs.

SKILLET HASH

The key to any great hash is to start with perfect potatoes, and our First Watch Potatoes (page 24) are just that. You could say they play well with friends. For an Italian flare, try our Parma. If you're a veggie lover, our Market is ideal. And, our most popular, the Farmhouse has bacon and fresh avocado. There's something for everyone.

SERVES 1

SKILLET HASH BASE RECIPE

1 tablespoon butter

1½ cups First Watch Potatoes (page 24)

½ tablespoon canola oil

Hash ingredients (see variations, pages 138 and 139)

2 eggs, cooked any style

Freshly chopped parsley, for garnish

Freshly chopped chives, for garnish

OPTIONAL ACCOMPANIMENTS

½ cup fresh fruit

1 thick slice whole-grain artisan toast

2 tablespoons all-natural preserves

1. Heat butter in a 10-inch nonstick pan. Add First Watch Potatoes, turning potatoes to brown on all sides.
2. Heat a nonstick 10-inch skillet over medium-high heat. Add oil and then hash ingredients.
3. After 1½ minutes, add First Watch Potatoes and sauté until all ingredients are hot, about 3 minutes.
4. Once ingredients are hot, mix in cheese and transfer to a large serving plate; keep warm.
5. In a buttered nonstick 8-inch skillet, cook eggs to desired doneness. Place over top of hash mixture.
6. Garnish with fresh herbs and serve with side of fresh fruit, whole-grain artisan toast and preserves.

PARMA HASH

2 tablespoons Roasted Tomatoes (page 32), diced

2 tablespoons Roasted Crimini Mushrooms (page 30)

1 tablespoon Roasted Onions (page 31)

½ cup cooked Italian sausage, crumbled

2 tablespoons mozzarella cheese, shredded

1 tablespoon Parmesan cheese, shredded

1. Add the above ingredients, except for cheese, in step 2 of the Skillet Hash Base recipe (page 137).
2. Top with cheeses before serving.

FARMHOUSE HASH

¼ cup crispy bacon, diced

2 tablespoons Roasted Tomatoes (page 32)

1 tablespoon Roasted Onions (page 31)

2 tablespoons cheddar jack cheese, shredded

4 avocado slices, for garnish

1. Add the above ingredients, except for cheese and avocado, in step 2 of the Skillet Hash Base recipe (page 137).
2. Top with fresh avocado slices before adding eggs.

MARKET HASH

2 tablespoons Roasted Zucchini (page 31)

2 tablespoons Roasted Crimini Mushrooms (page 30)

2 tablespoons roasted red peppers, drained and diced

¼ cup Roasted Shallots (page 32)

½ cup spinach leaves

2 tablespoons mozzarella cheese, shredded

¼ cup herbed goat cheese

1. Add the above ingredients, except for cheeses, in step 2 of the Skillet Hash base recipe (page 137).
2. Add mozzarella in step 3.
3. Top with herbed goat cheese before adding eggs.

JUICES & COFFEE

JUICE BAR

Juices are a natural extension of what we stand for at First Watch: fresh, simple, healthy and delicious. We make all of our juices fresh every morning. Each juice is a delicate balance of the ideal sweet to earthy to sour ratio. Flavor comes first. The health benefits are a great bonus.

When juicing at home, it all starts with the right juicer. Blenders and food processors are not great substitutes for juicers. There are two main types of juicers: masticating and centrifugal. Masticating works very slowly and doesn't generate much heat, which preserves the natural enzymes in the juice. But, it takes a long time. Centrifugal juicers have a series of blades that turn very quickly, so you can juice faster and juice a higher volume of ingredients.

KALE TONIC

MAKES ABOUT 2 (10-OUNCE) GLASSES

Our Kale Tonic is perfectly balanced—sweet yet earthy, delicious yet healthy. Kale has been popular in smoothies, but we decided to take it the fresh juice route. One sip in and you'll instantly know why it's one of our best-selling juices and stays on the menu year-round.

16 ounces fresh Fuji apple juice

1 ounce fresh kale juice

2 ounces fresh English cucumber juice

2 ounces fresh lemon juice

1 Place all ingredients in a glass and whisk until thoroughly combined.

2 Enjoy immediately or transfer to an airtight container and store in the refrigerator.

DAY GLOW

MAKES ABOUT 2 (10-OUNCE) GLASSES

This kicked-up orange juice was the first juice we ever debuted on our menus. Ginger adds a little spice and bite, but the naturally sweet carrots and oranges are the true stars. Drink this and you're sure to feel a healthy glow all day.

- 12 ounces fresh carrot juice
- 12 ounces orange juice
- 2 ounces lemon juice
- 2 teaspoons ginger juice

1 Place all ingredients in a glass and whisk until thoroughly combined.
2 Enjoy immediately or transfer to an airtight container and store in the refrigerator.

MORNING MEDITATION

MAKES ABOUT 2 (10-OUNCE) GLASSES

This is a fan favorite, which almost says it all. As beautiful as it is delicious, this juice has vibrant contrasting colors with a layer of orange, lemon and turmeric and then beet juice on top.

8 ounces orange juice

1½ ounces lemon juice

1 tablespoon fresh turmeric juice

1½ ounces agave nectar

1 tablespoon ginger juice

8 ounces cold filtered water

2 ounces fresh beet juice, divided

1 Place all ingredients except beet juice in a glass and whisk until thoroughly combined.
2 Refrigerate in an airtight container until ready to serve.
3 To serve, add ice to a glass, pour mixture into glass and top with 1 ounce (2 tablespoons) beet juice per glass.

STRAWBERRY SMASH

MAKES ABOUT 2 (10-OUNCE) GLASSES

Think of this juice as a grown-up strawberry lemonade. We juice our strawberries in-house and cut their sweetness with bright, fresh lemons. Needless to say, it's nothing like the 25-cent lemonade stands from childhood.

4 ounces fresh strawberry juice

8 ounces cold water

4 ounces simple syrup

4 ounces fresh lemon juice

1. Place all ingredients in a glass and whisk until thoroughly combined.
2. Enjoy immediately or transfer to an airtight container and store in the refrigerator.

CHILLED PEAR CIDER

MAKES ABOUT 2 (10-OUNCE) GLASSES

The Chilled Pear Cider is like fall in a glass. We combine the natural sweetness of pears and apples with a slight bite from the ginger juice and finish it with the bright acidity of lemon. Every sip will have you celebrating the season.

- 12 ounces fresh red Anjou pear juice
- 6 ounces fresh Fuji apple juice
- 2 ounces fresh lemon juice
- 1 ounce ginger juice

1. Place all ingredients in a glass and whisk until thoroughly combined.
2. Enjoy immediately or transfer to an airtight container and store in the refrigerator.

COFFEE MATTERS

Coffee is a big deal at First Watch. That's why we put a whole pot on your table right when you order it. And that's why, from the day in 1983 when we opened the original First Watch, we've sought out the best coffee beans available and brewed them to exacting specifications. Yeah, we've always been coffee geeks.

We tasted and researched coffee from around the world before deciding to source our beans from small, independent farms in the Huila ("Wee-luh") region of Colombia. Many of the farmers are women who are heads of household, and they handpick the beans on hillside plots of three to four acres. Through First Watch's Project Sunrise, we partner with them to support sustainable businesses that elevate the lives of their families and improve conditions in their rural communities.

The Huila region's soil, altitude and climate are ideal for growing coffee with a flavor profile that is rich and complex, with just a touch of sweetness that makes it the perfect accompaniment for food, especially breakfast, brunch and lunch.

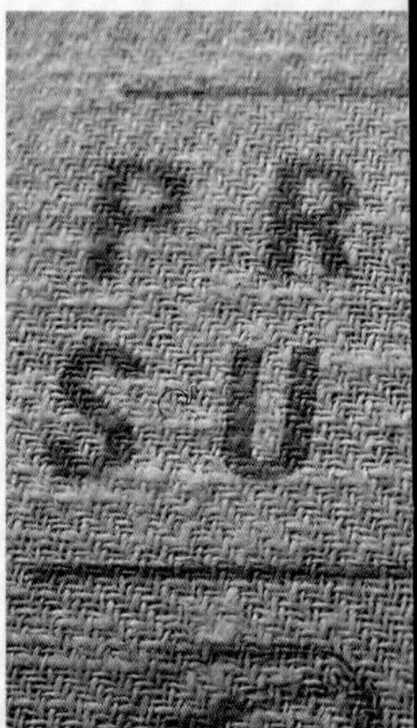

Everyone has a favorite way of making coffee at home. But to come as close as possible to the First Watch version:

- Buy a bag of Project Sunrise coffee at First Watch.
- Use filtered water.
- Follow the tried-and-true proportions for an ideal cup — 1 heaping tablespoon of ground coffee per 6 ounces of water.

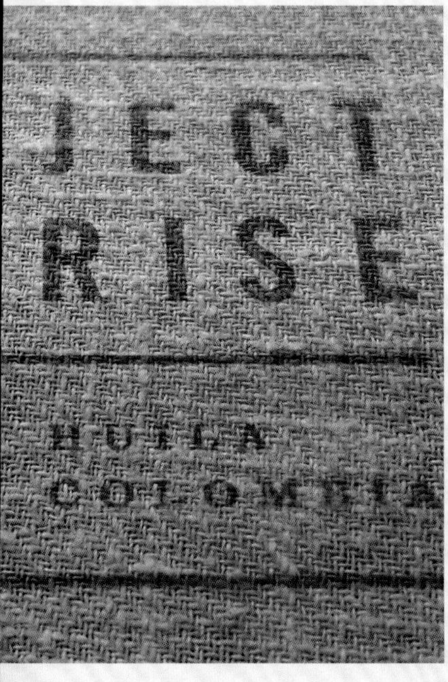

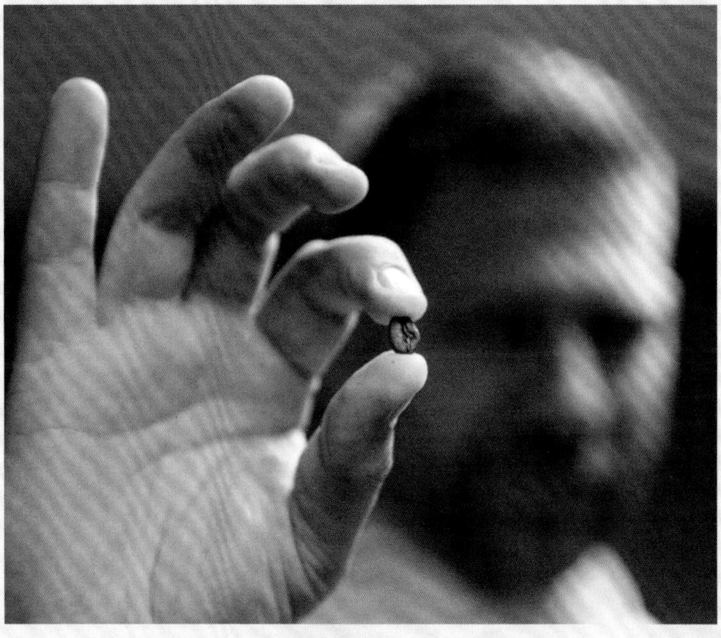

DAYTIME CAFE
FIRST WATCH

INDEX

Italicized page numbers indicate photos.

- F -

- G -

- H -